More Praise for
The Ten Things to Do When Your Life Falls Apart

"Practical guidelines to turn a heartbreak or tragedy into a valuable transition to a more fulfilling, richer life."
— Terry Cole-Whittaker, author of *Live Your Bliss*

"Daphne Rose Kingma has been my guide through some of the most challenging times of my life. Now, for the first time, she shares the wisdom I've counted on for decades. If the storms of life are ravaging you, this is the book you need by your side."
— M. J. Ryan, author of
AdaptAbility: How to Survive Change You Didn't Ask For
and *Attitudes of Gratitude*

"A no-nonsense, yet compassionate, guide. Invaluable for those going through crisis or handling challenges of any kind! (And who is not?)"
— Sue Patton Thoele, author of
The Mindful Woman and *The Courage to Be Yourself*

THE TEN THINGS
TO DO WHEN YOUR
LIFE FALLS APART

Also by Daphne Rose Kingma

Coming Apart

365 Days of Love

True Love

Finding True Love

Loving Yourself

The Men We Never Knew

The Future of Love

THE TEN THINGS
TO DO WHEN YOUR
LIFE FALLS APART

An Emotional and
Spiritual Handbook

Daphne Rose Kingma

New World Library
Novato, California

For
otto
with love and gratitude

New World Library
14 Pamaron Way
Novato, California 94949

Text design by Mary Ann Casler

Library of Congress Cataloging-in-Publication Data
Kingma, Daphne Rose.
The ten things to do when your life falls apart : an emotional and spiritual handbook / Daphne Rose Kingma.
   p.   cm.
ISBN 978-1-57731-698-5 (pbk. : alk. paper)
1. Adjustment (Psychology) 2. Adjustment (Psychology)—Religious aspects. 3. Suffering. I. Title.
BF335.K54 2010
155.9'3—dc22   2010001049

First printing, April 2010
ISBN 978-1-57731-698-5
Printed in Canada on 100% postconsumer-waste recycled paper

g New World Library is a proud member of the Green Press Initiative.

10 9 8 7 6 5 4

CONTENTS

When Life Falls Apart

"Human beings are not helpless. They have never been helpless.
They have only been deflected or deceived or dispirited.
So long as people have a vision of life as it ought
to be...they can look at the world with...confidence."

— Norman Cousins

If you've picked up this book, it's probably because in one way or another — or in a whole lot of ways — it feels as if your life is falling apart and you're looking for some answers.

First, take comfort in the fact that you are not alone. I was reminded once again of how complicated and difficult life has gotten when I ran into my friend Jane the other day. She was looking a little harried as she stood in line at Jeannine's, our local coffee bar.

When I asked her how she was, she said, "Fine. Aside from the fact that my entire life is falling apart."

She ordered a latte, then went on to say that her boyfriend of six years had just announced that he'd fallen in love with another woman. Her landlord had given her a thirty-day notice — after living in Europe for three years, his son had just returned to the United States and would be needing her apartment. Her job as a school librarian was being axed as a consequence of educational budget cuts. She'd caught her fourteen-year-old daughter smoking dope, then her eighty-three-year-old mother was diagnosed with Alzheimer's — the diagnosis coming a week before Jane was going to send her daughter to live with her mom so the purple-haired girl could get a taste of some good old-fashioned stability.

"I think I'm coping," she sighed. "But sometimes I feel like a terrible person, as if somehow I should have been able to avoid all this. And the worst thing is I keep wondering if there's any meaning to all this, and if and when I'll ever again have a sense of happiness and peace."

Like Jane, a lot of us have been going through what feels like exceptionally hard times. Indeed, the phrase "my entire life feels out of control" is not just humorous hyperbole but refers to startling new levels of challenge. We know how to handle ordinary problems. They are vexing and inconvenient and take our time and energy, but they don't throw us into emotional or spiritual turmoil. A crisis, on the other hand, leads us into emotional waters where we feel in over our head, and it calls upon us to explore unfamiliar spiritual terrain.

When hardship hits, especially when a bunch of things pile on all at once, we can be shaken to the core, and life feels completely out of control. Just as when the brakes suddenly go out on a winding mountain road, the problems you're facing now may seem to have come flying in out of nowhere. Whatever they are, you have to act quickly, often in ways that are improvised and unfamiliar. You find yourself experiencing emotions you have never felt before, attempting solutions you never imagined having to contemplate, and responding with behaviors that seem fastened together with psychological duct tape.

When life throws us a curveball, our first response is shock, denial, and disbelief. We can't believe that this — or all of this — is actually happening. Once we digest the fact that it really is happening and that it won't go away, we begin to bargain, to try to manage the unwieldy monster. Maybe it'll change tomorrow. Maybe my wife was just threatening — she'll be back. Maybe the bank miscalculated the dividends. Maybe the hospital got the X-rays mixed up. In this deeply painful emotional state, we're torn between facing the truth of what has occurred and still hoping against hope that somehow the nightmare will be repealed.

But when bargaining no longer works, then what? How do you mend your heart after loss? How do you carry on or begin again? What can you do when your wife walks out? Your child dies? Your husband takes you to custody court and "buys" the right to move your children six states away? How can you keep on reaching for your dreams when your efforts keep coming to naught? When you come back shattered from a war? When every cent you squirreled away has vanished in WallStreetspeak and cybersmoke, and at age sixty-four with a PhD you find yourself, weirdly, working as a paint consultant at a hardware store?

More than ever before, we're all in the soup together. And yet, no matter how many other people are going through their own version of a seemingly out-of-control life, it's still devastating when it's happening to you.

This book is about those times when life has become so overwhelmingly difficult that you feel as if you want to give up — when it feels as if you can no longer cope, when you feel as if you've been taxed to the max. On an emotional level you're wondering how you'll make it through all the terrible feelings: grief, loss, sadness, despair. But from a deeper spiritual intelligence, you may find yourself asking, "How can I deal with what's happening to me in a better way? What is the meaning of all this?"

Every life has such seasons. But now, because of world-encompassing natural and financial catastrophes, vast numbers of people around the globe are facing similar difficulties. Some people think that astrologers or psychics can foresee such events, map them out for us, and tie their timing to the stars or our past-life actions so we can somehow avoid them. But the truth is that no one escapes such things, no matter what their origins. Loss, heartache, tragedy, and strings of difficult events that leave us breathless with confusion, terrified about the future, hating our lives, and wondering about their meaning are the warp and weft of the fabric of the human condition. No matter your birth sign, hair color, nationality of origin, net taxable income, or acts of a thousand past lives — no one is exempt. So long as there are people on earth, such things will continue to occur.

In the past, when times were easier, we could cope by externalizing our problems and their solutions. If you didn't feel good about yourself, you could tell yourself it was because you didn't have the great Louis Vuitton suitcase, a better car, or the investment portfolio that could guarantee a cushy retirement. If you had relationship issues, you could imagine that they were about the other person — you just hadn't found the perfect person, or the person you'd found wasn't meeting all your needs, so best find yourself another one.

Now, though, it seems that our problems are coming in so close and hitting us so hard that we can't project them outward anymore. They're in our households, under our roofs, in our checkbooks, and in our hearts, and we have no choice but to deal with them. Our traditional methods of problem solving have been to try harder to regain control, and so, as we face what's happening now, our first impulse is to look over our shoulders and do more of what we did then.

When these techniques don't seem to work, we get panicky. We want to regain control, to have life magically restored to the way it was before the crisis — before the divorce, before the crash in the stock market, before the flood, before losing the house to foreclosure. But when life falls apart, we have to learn a new way. The call is to deal with our challenges in ways that are fresh, authentic, and deep, that touch at the core of ourselves. We need to create not just another bailout but a true sense of meaning. And that's what this book is about.

This book is not for sissies. It's not about how to deal with the ordinary, garden-variety upsets of life — missed flights that louse up your schedule, wrinkles and bad-hair days that send you running to the internet for new shampoos and face creams. It's about coping with the really tough stuff and finding the way through.

We need to learn how to do this because, as well as innumerable blessings, beauties, and moments of mystery and grandeur, life holds sequences of loss and tragedy that shock us, test our mettle, and leave us wondering how we'll ever regain a sense of wholeness and whether there's any guiding hand whatsoever in the universe.

It's Not Your Fault; It's Your Journey

I write all this not as one who has led a charmed life but as a fellow traveler. In the past two years, along with enjoying life's many blessings, I also moved my house (twice) and my office (twice), was in a major car accident, had my computer stolen, ended a ten-year romantic relationship, had a severe physical injury, lost my 10,000-person mailing list at the hands of a careless webmaster and my share of acorns in the national financial fracas, was audited by the IRS, and started a new consulting practice. Some of these things happened one at a time, with little pauses in between; a lot of them came rolling down the pike one after another like cars at the Indianapolis Speedway. Like anyone else, when these things happened, I felt wildly unprepared. That's because when hard times strike and you don't have the answers, you can't help but feel caught off guard. You keep asking yourself, How can this be happening to me? Why didn't I buy sand bags? Get my money out of Madoff? Sell my house? Notice my husband was having an affair? Take my kid to the doctor when he complained about all those headaches?

All this blame and self-judgment springs from two assumptions: one, that we should be smart and capable enough to prevent such terrible things from happening to us, and two, that we should be able to meet any challenge and solve every problem that arises. But we're not gods. Difficulties teach us, among other things, that we're not in control, at least not completely, and that the ways in which we've handled our lives up till now may not be enough. In fact, part of the purpose of crisis is to get us to stretch in new and completely different ways. Major life events are profound opportunities for emotional healing and spiritual development.

That's easy to say, I know, but not as easy to do. The process can be frightening and hard to go through. So what can I tell you, at this anguishing turning point of your life? I can tell you, first of all, that you will get through it. Life is holding you. Life wants you here; otherwise, you wouldn't still be here, asking these questions and looking for answers. Something, a force larger than you, the force that is you, is inviting you to change. How do you know that? Because you're in pain. And the presence of pain is the promise of change. That's because it hurts to suffer, and when we're suffering we're far more inclined to take risks, to take action, to fall on our knees, to break out of bad habits, to break out of the box in order to get beyond the pain that we're in. Suffering, therefore, is always an invitation to change, to get into alignment with what is most true and beautiful in life, with our deepest and most expansive feelings, with Love itself.

It may not feel this way right now, but just as the oak tree, folded and invisible, lies whole within the acorn, so everything you need to live through this current anguish is within you. You are blessed. Your life is designed. If this crisis weren't meant to be part of your life, it would not be happening. This is the moment and these are precisely the experiences through which your emotional body is being healed, your soul is being refined and enlarged, and your life itself is taking on a new meaning.

A Hand to Hold

For twenty-five years I've been writing books to guide people through various kinds of suffering — for folks anguishing over whether or not they'll ever be able to find a person to love (*Finding True Love*); for people wondering if they'll ever recover from a relationship breakup (*Coming Apart*); for seekers trying to understand the meaning of the massive divorce rates and shocking upheavals in the fabric of our relationships (*The Future of Love*); for women wanting to get closer in their intimate relationships to men, that mysterious gender (*The Men We Never Knew*); and for those desiring to live a life of depth, creativity, and inspiration (*365 Days of Love*).

People all over the world have turned to me for consolation, direction, and insight about their emotional anguish, their relationship issues, their creativity, and their spiritual lives. In these difficult times, people are reaching out to me more than ever before, asking for help in understanding the deeper meaning of the struggles that they're going through. That's because, instinctively, we're all beginning to recognize that it's time for deeper, soul-level solutions and that these are only going to come from within ourselves. Although we still want — and need — to understand our difficulties from an emotional point of view, we also want to look at them from a spiritual perspective, to see the larger truth that they may hold for us.

Over the years, it has been my privilege to shepherd a great many people through the delicate terrain that lies between our emotional and spiritual selves, to show the profound connection between them and how they operate in our daily lives and sufferings. It is my privilege, now, to hold your hand as you go through your present difficult circumstances.

The Ten Things

Last fall a dear friend of mine came to visit me from Europe. His life had just folded in on itself. He'd lost his job. His wife had left him. His financial portfolio had dwindled to less than a third of its original size. On a moment's notice, he'd had to move from the apartment he'd moved into just six months before, and he'd been diagnosed with a slow-moving degenerative disease that would, ultimately, be fatal. He was in need of deep comfort as well as distraction from his anguish.

I did my best to provide both. We sat in the garden and had picnic lunches; we walked and hiked. We went to a concert, an art gallery opening, a party; we had dinner at an outside café and dinner with friends. We went to a Buddhist temple and prayed. He wept. He regretted. He agonized. He wondered.

Finally, one afternoon as we were coming down from a hike in the mountains, he said to me, "Daphne, before I go home, will you make me a list of the ten things I need to do to get through this crisis?" My foot tripped on a protruding branch. That's a lot to ask, I thought to myself. That's practically like asking me to write a book.

We came home. I sat down. Within minutes I had made a list. It was for him. It is for you. It's for all of us.

These ten things — and I don't care what you call them: ways, steps, practices, teachings — are things to do, to stop doing, to think of, to remember, and to become so that you can find your way through this very hard time. Their purpose is to show you that rather than being random assaults from an uncaring universe, the difficulties you are going through have meaning and purpose. Not only is your crisis here to get you to exercise your coping muscles, and therein to discover your strength; your problems also have a larger purpose. And that is to remind you of the quality of being that you truly are — powerful, loving, eternal.

Each of The Ten is a way of turning the lens of your life so you can catch more of the light that is always available for healing. As you engage with them, one by one, they will move you back and forth between the emotional and spiritual levels, interweaving the two like the luminous strands of your DNA. Taken together, they represent nothing less than a spiritual practice that will result in a subtle restructuring of your psyche, a reshaping of your consciousness in a spiritual direction.

It seems that it shouldn't be so hard to respond to real-life challenges from a spiritual point of view. After all, for a couple decades now, we've been tossing around the notion that we are "spiritual beings having a human experience." But coming to terms with the full meaning of those words — with what it means to abide day by day in the deep space that is, in fact, our spiritual nature — is something with which most of us still don't have a lot of experience. In terms of our collective spiritual development, we're more like a bunch of spoiled teenagers having a casual summer romance with our spiritual maturity, while at the same time we're hanging on to all the things we've always loved, the material-world free-for-all — the toys, the stuff, the wildly exaggerated promises of complete emotional fulfillment, the internet techno-magical-mystery tour that offers us virtual versions of almost everything we can dream of.

Part of us has always wanted to understand the larger truth of our lives — why we're here, whether there's a point to all this. But we haven't always known what the path to that understanding might be. At times it may have seemed confusing or way too hard to follow; at other times we've found ourselves wondering whether there even was a path. But when circumstances bring us to our knees, we're finally willing to tiptoe into the exploration of who we really are and what our lives might really be about. We're ready to come into the presence of the beauty, the grandeur, the breathtaking power of our own true nature — which, at the end of the day, is nothing more nor less than the embodiment of all-encompassing Love.

Coming to terms with this truth in times of unbearable anguish, connecting with it when your world is careening out of control and you're scared to death — that is the promise of The Ten. It is my hope that they will help to heal your heart, awaken your soul, and deliver you to the liberation that occurs when you understand the larger meaning of your life.

The chapters that follow are a guide to finding emotional and spiritual balance in the midst of crisis.

Reading them is a little like dining at a smorgasbord. You can read them in the order they're offered and find that you move through them to a state of peaceful conclusion. Or you can read them one at a time, letting your hand fall on a page or your mind call you to exactly the chapter you need at the moment. Whatever your method, my deep prayer is that in making the passage you will find the spiritual equanimity that can transform your life.

Come now, let us begin.

If you want to get through this crisis,
you will have to

Cry Your Heart Out

CHAPTER I

Cry Your Heart Out

"He who sits in the house of grief will eventually sit in the garden."

— Hafiz

Hard times, more than any others, reveal to us the truth that the signature of our humanity is our emotional nature. What differentiates us from stones and butterflies is the degree to which what happens to us affects us on an emotional level. We don't just experience things — get a divorce, lose our house, watch our dog die from eating poison — we have feelings about these events. It is the depth and nuance of our feelings — of our joy, sorrow, anger, and fear — that give texture to our humanity.

Sorrow and grief are the emotions that apply when we experience loss, and crying is the body's mechanism for expressing grief. It may seem self-evident that we should cry when we're in pain, but it's surprising how much we resist our tears. Often it is only when we've been overtaken by them that we finally discover how terribly aggrieved we are.

We live in a culture that's afraid of grieving; we don't know how to cry. When our lives fall apart in one way or another, we usually try to take control of things and solve them, forget them, or deny them — rather than experience them, accept them, or see the meaning they may hold for us. That's because underlying many of our responses to difficulty is the unstated assumption that we should be able to engage in life, liberty, and the unbridled pursuit of happiness without ever having to grieve — over anything. It's almost as if we believe that pain, suffering, and challenge are bad and should never be a part of our path.

The truth is that pain is one of our greatest teachers, hurt can be a birth, and our sufferings are the portals to change. This being true, we need to know how to grieve, to mourn, to shed our tears, because grief is the cure for the pain of loss. Tears are the medicine of grieving.

When life is hard, when you're in a crisis, you

should cry not because you're weak but because crying holds the power of healing. Tears, in fact, are the vehicle for transformation. When you cry, your loss moves through you to the point of exit. What was holding you up and eating you up, what was stuck inside your body, gets released and moves outside your body. Your physical structure is quite literally cleansed and, like a blackboard sponged clean, is available to receive the imprint of whatever wants to come next. That's why, when you have cried, you will be reborn, free to begin again.

Hard Afternoons on the Couch

It has been clinically demonstrated that when you suppress sadness you also suppress positive emotions. What we don't feel on one end of the emotional spectrum, we don't feel on the other. As a consequence, people who try to be happy all the time, who suppress what they perceive to be the "negative" emotions of sorrow and grief, actually, over time, become more anxious and depressed. Crying is not a sign of weakness; we shouldn't staunch our tears. They're a healing balm, a river to the future.

I don't know about you, but I've had a bunch of really great cries in my life — days, afternoons, and nights when I took to the couch or my bed and literally wailed about the hardships of life. I've cried over sweethearts who left, lovers I couldn't get rid of, bad decisions, feeling forsaken by God, people who didn't "get" me, wrecking my dancing shoes, selling my house, feeling isolated, wretched, and unloved, and feeling the impending sorrow of death. I have cried because of my stupidity, my naïveté, and my lack of courage, because of tornadoes and earthquakes, because of money I lost and money that was stolen from me (a lot of both).

At times I've been surprised by the magnitude of my tears, by the amount of sheer wailing and letting go that certain circumstances called for. I've been shocked, almost worried that such a big cry might have been some sort of hysterical emotional excess, some kind of performance. But the quiet integration, the fragile and yet sublime peace that followed each vintage cry was the measure of the healing power of those tears.

I've always felt better because of having cried. I have felt reglued, reborn, strong, silken, vulnerable, permeable, powerful, radical, formidable, tender, pure, loving, exquisite, invincible, clear, new, real, whole.

When you stop and think about it, there are things worth crying about every day. So cry, for God's sake. Cry your heart out.

Grief as Suicide Prevention

On that note, I used to have a friend who once said to me with envy, "You cry easy." She was going through a very difficult time, facing the institutionalization of the young Down syndrome son she had hoped to be able to keep at home. When she told me, in vivid detail, about visiting the facility, seeing the room in which her little boy would likely spend the rest of his life, I was moved to tears. I unabashedly wept as we sat together having our nice lunch at a very spiffy restaurant, while across from me she sat stone-faced and brave, "keeping it all together."

Years passed, and we lost touch. Then one afternoon, she called me from the psych ward of her local hospital. Some very tough things had happened, she told me, and as a consequence, she'd tried to kill herself. When she found herself still alive, the morning after they'd pumped out her stomach, she found herself crying for hours. "I guess the dam finally broke," she said. "I must have a ton of crying to do. Years' worth."

I've always told the people I work with that if you don't cry teaspoonfuls, you will cry bucketfuls, and that's in part what my friend confirmed. Our bodies and our hearts, the elaborate museums where all our unexpressed emotions are stored, are designed to have experiences, feel what they feel about them, and then release those feelings. If we don't, they gather like leaves in rain gutters, clogging the downspout until, finally, the rain gushes over the edge and falls in sheets in front of the living room windows.

My friend had to go to the brink of death to find her tears. Maybe you can start crying now.

The Golden Shawl

I have another friend named Mari. After not seeing her for a long time, I ran into her a couple of years ago at a meditation retreat we both often attend. A lovely woman in her forties who is a teacher of the healing arts, she brings balance to everyone around her, but this time when we met, she seemed suddenly, quietly older. There were thickets of lines around her eyes, deep new creases around her mouth.

When I asked how she'd been since we'd last seen each other, Mari told me that it had been a very hard year. Without any warning, her fifteen-year-old daughter had died. She'd had an allergic reaction to an herbal energy potion she'd taken two times before, gone into anaphylactic shock, and died within minutes. Telling me all this, Mari started crying, and seeing her, I did too. We stood there on the paradoxically very brightly colored carpet of the hotel lobby where the retreat was being held, crying together for quite a few minutes. Finally, she reached in her purse, took out a Kleenex, and wiped her eyes. "Thanks," she said, "it's so good to cry." She told me her friends were tired of her crying. The death had been six months ago, and they wondered why she was still "so affected."

I didn't see Mari for almost six months after that. When we met again at the next retreat, she looked softer, ravaged, beautiful in a different new way. I could see that in the time that had passed she had somehow become larger than her grief, that she had encompassed it. I was deeply moved when I saw how big she had become around it.

When I asked her how she was doing, she told me that she was doing somewhat better. She told me that while everybody close to her still seemed to think that she should be "over it" by now, she wasn't. She went on to say that, with several other mothers of children who had died, she'd formed a grieving group; when any of them felt the pain starting to become unbearable, they'd call all the others and get together to have "a crying time."

She said, "We just sit together in one of our living rooms, and cry our hearts out for a while. And then when we're all cried out, we say good-bye and go on with our lives again."

I ran into Mari at the lunch break later that day. There was a bazaar being held in the lobby of the hotel, with vendors selling a lot of beautiful things. Mari had found an exquisite ochre shawl, and I stepped up just as she was trying it on. She asked me if I thought she should buy it. I told her I thought it looked lovely with her brown eyes and dark hair, and that maybe now she could treat herself to something beautiful.

When I saw her later that afternoon, the golden shawl was wrapped around her. Mari looked gorgeous and she was smiling.

Grief is a long and complicated journey, and getting to the golden shawl part of the story always takes a lot of tears. That's because anything short of real grieving leaves you with the pain still stuck like a chicken bone in your throat. You will never get to the equanimity that follows grief by avoiding the grief — by thinking the loss will go away, pretending you weren't affected, rationalizing, trying to talk yourself out of the pain: "I should be over it by now. I don't know why I'm so upset. What's the matter with me, anyway?"

We ask ourselves these ridiculous questions because in this easy-way-out culture of ours we've been behaving for a very long time as if we could avoid things, as if we could go around our difficulties instead of going through them. It doesn't work that way. What hurts will not simply "go away." You will not just "get over it." Tears are the way you make room for the birth that follows grief. They are one of the true and beautiful pathways through the pain. In fact, they are the royal road to emotional healing.

It's been said that when we cry, when the tears wash down the sides of our faces, we are brought back into the cellular memory of having our faces bathed in amniotic fluid, taken back to the bliss we felt in the womb. This is one of the reasons why crying is so profoundly healing. We are literally brought back to the state we were in before we were born. When we allow ourselves to be bathed in the cleansing elixir of our tears, we clean the slate, we return to birth. In newness there is always hope. When things are new we know we can begin again.

That is why, once we have cried, we often feel, quite literally, reborn.

For Those Who Suffer in Our Midst

It's not just for ourselves that we have reason to cry. There is so much suffering in the world that we could build a wailing wall around it and just weep nonstop for the pain of us all, until all of us are healed.

Take, for instance, the fact that the United States has 5 percent of the world's population and 25 percent of its incarcerated criminals, and that it spends $68 billion per year on "corrections." In California alone, the state prison budget is over $11 billion, and it costs more than $50,000 per year to house an inmate, more than the annual cost of an education at Yale, Princeton, or Harvard.

The tragedy of this was brought home to me in a personal way a number of years ago when I made the acquaintance of Roy, a murderer in prison. He had written a letter to a magazine in which he said that as a young man his unaddressed anger had ultimately expressed itself in taking another person's life, but he now realized his anger had been a compensation for his deep grief over the many devastating losses he'd experienced. I was moved by his very articulate awareness that, as for so many men, his anger was a cover for his grief. A few days later, using the address he included in his letter to the magazine, I sent him a copy of a book I had written about men and their emotions in which I had addressed this very issue.

Months passed. I hadn't imagined I would ever hear from him, and by the time he wrote back, I'd practically forgotten that I'd sent him the book. In his note, he explained that prisoners were not allowed to receive unsolicited books from any outside source; since my book had arrived out of the blue, it had required a special hearing to decide whether or not he could, in fact, receive it.

In the end, the prison officials had allowed him to accept the book. He'd read it, he told me, and wept, wishing that as a young man of seventeen he had heard about or understood the things it said. He wrote unself-pityingly to me about his life. His own father died when he was four, leaving him alone with his mother, a slightly dull-witted but very pretty woman. She went through a series of boyfriends, the first of whom raped her. This led to the birth of a little sister, whom Roy came to adore, but she died of meningitis when she was three and he was seven. There was a series of other stepfathers after that, each of whom hung around for a while before taking off. Finally, one stepfather chose to stay with the family and provide for them, and Roy started to find solace and direction with him. Then, during a family picnic at the lake one summer afternoon, Roy watched helpless from the shore as, flailing and screaming for rescue in the distance, his stepfather drowned.

Wild with the loss of her daughter and her husband, Roy's mother leaned on him to become the provider. He was by then fifteen. Dropping out of school, he became an apprentice carpenter, and one night two years later, the second time he'd ever been out drinking in a bar, a gang member six inches taller than he was roughed him up and threatened him with a knife. When the gang member hurled the knife in his direction, Roy grabbed it from the floor, and with the tragic irony of uncalculated precision, stabbed his assailant between the ribs and directly into his heart. Within minutes the other young man was dead; within a year Roy was sentenced to sixty to ninety years in prison.

Roy has become a writer and a Buddhist in prison. He tells me that his cell is his monastery, that life "inside" is his spiritual path. "Unlike you," he wrote to me humorously once, "I always have plenty of time to write." In the several years I've known him, he's started a periodical and finished two books.

Once when I was flying across the country to make

a speech, I took a few side flights and stopped to visit him. I stayed overnight in a plain, small visitors' motel not far from the prison. It was a sunny day when I awoke the next morning, and I decided to take a walk before the afternoon visiting time. As I walked through the town I realized that the streets were lined on either side with prisons. Young men, many of them high school age, mostly brown and black, but among them a smattering of white, were playing ball in the prison yard, the arc of their lives already drawn, their chances, for the most part, already over.

It was late afternoon when it was time for my visit. I wore a white dress. I was early, and before I went in I walked twice around the barbed-wire, razor coil–encrusted prison yard fence, weeping with each step and waving at the prisoners who stood outside on the steps here and there, waving poignantly back at me.

As I walked, I wondered if they had ever cried for themselves, or if anyone had ever cried over them. I thought, too, what if we could create a ministry of tears? What if we consecrated some time in each of our days to weep, first for ourselves, but then also for each of these ones whose lives have been broken — who in the vast wholeness that is all of our humanity have been assigned the life's work of being criminals, while we are privileged to have been born of parents and in circumstances that, in spite of our individual rations of pain, allow us to live as free men and women? What healing would happen? What peace would reign? How much would our differences dissolve? And what would we learn about the true nature of love?

☙ You and Your Tears ❧

Here are some questions to answer as you contemplate the healing role of grief and tears in your life. Perhaps you've never been aware that crying, along with being a spilling over of feeling, actually has a curative effect. It is not a mistake; it is a necessity. Bearing this in mind, you can use these questions to help shepherd you on your own healing journey.

- What's the old ache in your heart that you've never wept over? Something that happened in your childhood, that you've talked yourself out of crying about? Something other people told you that you shouldn't cry over? Something that happened last week? The death of your dog? The loss of your job? Devastating words from your boss? Cutting remarks from your son or daughter? The $200 raise in your rent? The client who just ripped you off?

- What is unbearable in your current circumstances that you've tried to solve and get a grip on, but if you stop and think about it is really so unbearably painful that you should just have a good cry over it? Who would you choose to be with you when you shed these tears? Where would you go to cry — to the ocean? To a listener, a priest? To the cathedral inside your own heart? Wherever that place is for you, I urge you to name it now, and go there, and let your fine tears set you on the journey of your healing. And if one good cry doesn't do it, how can you give yourself the time and space to cry as often as you need to?

- If you were to offer your tears as a ministry of compassion, for whom would you offer your tears? For what cause? Is there anything else, once you have finished with crying, that you'd like to do on behalf of these suffering others?

If you want to get through this crisis,
you will have to

Face Your Defaults

CHAPTER 2

Face Your Defaults

"Awareness in itself is curative."

— Fritz Perls

Your defaults are whatever you do when you don't know how to cope or what to do next. On your computer, your defaults are what show up when you haven't specifically programmed it for anything else. In life your defaults are the coping mechanisms you revert to when you're too scared to risk trying anything new.

Defaults are habitual behaviors, and they're not always the best way to cope. New — and especially, difficult — circumstances howl out for new solutions:

improvisation, imagination, ingenuity. But when we're intimidated, scared, and overwhelmed, most of us resort to our default behaviors because, well, we always have, and there they are.

In theory, there may be nothing wrong with your defaults. In the right circumstances, they can be great strategies. It's great to have a nose-to-the-grindstone work ethic when you're working on a project that has to be finished in three days. It's wonderful to talk endlessly to your friends about the ever-unfolding tidal wave of issues in your romantic relationship, or to have a snack or a drink when a devastating disappointment leaves you reeling. But if you always do this or, more importantly, if you *only* do this — or if you do it to excess — especially when radically altered circumstances are crying out for different choices, you are living your life, well, by default.

The problem with defaults is that they're not tailored to the current situation. They're outdated, moss-covered, moth-eaten, and frayed. You've done them so long they're practically part of your DNA. Depressed? Head for the refrigerator. Lost your job? Have sixteen martinis. Brokenhearted? Blame yourself (instead of the unconscious cretin you took up with) for everything that went wrong. Hit a wall with a creative project? Throw in the towel and bemoan your lack of talent instead of expecting the inspiration that could helicopter in from left field.

Normal, garden-variety coping mechanisms can become defaults over time precisely because at first they seem to work. In the initial blush of excitement at their astonishing effectiveness, we may even feel we have a certain genius for problem solving. But over time, as you keep applying these adaptive behaviors, and especially if you become overly reliant on them, they lose their ability to do anything except repeat themselves. I remember practically seeing God the first time I smoked a cigarette. When I was in college I thought smoking was the greatest diet method ever, and the greatest brain-focusing drug (along with coffee) that I would ever come across. But wrangling loose from the noose of nicotine after it had become my default coping mechanism was one of the longest, toughest walks of my life.

Like smoking, a lot of default behaviors can become destructive traps:

- More than one hundred million prescriptions for antidepressants will be written this year, and more than one-third of the population consider themselves depressed (i.e., we are depressed as hell and not facing our feelings).

- Ten million people in the United States are now considered morbidly obese. Of them, three hundred thousand people die of obesity-related causes and over a hundred thousand people receive gastric bypass surgery annually. And one in five four-year-olds is now considered clinically obese (i.e., we are eating ourselves to death).

- One in thirteen adults in the United States is an alcoholic (i.e., we are drinking ourselves into oblivion).

If, when times are tough, you don't really examine your defaults, you will mindlessly apply them. Not only will nothing new come to pass, but chances are there will also be some dire consequences. In other words: Nothing new will ever happen if you keep doing the same old things.

Conversely, when you face your defaults, there's an instant influx of energy because you recognize that you are taking a first step on the path that can alter your situation. Emotionally, you're relieved when you are living in the truth; spiritually, you can trust that the cosmos will support you when you are living from your core. At the deepest levels of your being, you know who you are and what you really ought to be doing, and you know it isn't just the same old thing. Facing the behaviors that you might prefer to ignore will give you hope because you will know that, finally, you are moving in the direction of taking the actions that can change your life.

The Many Faces of Defaults

I often write in coffee shops, and lately I've noticed that a lot of the people who step up to the counter to order their morning coffee and tea, their bagels and pastries, are probably fifty to a hundred pounds overweight. I don't know why they're overweight, and I'm not judging, but it does make me wonder if overeating is slowly becoming humanity's default behavior. In Australia they've redesigned toilets to accommodate the approximately one hundred extra pounds the majority of Australians are now carrying. And I know that airlines, too, have designed bigger seats to accommodate the extra girth that a lot of passengers seem to have acquired. I wonder if soon there'll be Large-, Grande-, and Venti-sized coffins to accommodate the supersized bodies that we seem to be cultivating instead of dealing more directly with the heartbreaking challenges of our lives.

Obesity is just one of the signs that our bodies are literally carrying the weight of our sorrows instead of telegraphing our hope, our strength, and our well-being. But there are a number of other behaviors not so physically obvious but just as undermining that many of us use to manage the inescapable hardships of life.

THE RESCUER

One of my clients, a man in his mid-fifties named Bill, finally had the courage to face his defaults. A successful software company owner, Bill had a penchant for "rescuing" women. In his better moments, he called it "mentoring," and in truth, many of the women he dated went on to become very successful in their own right. He gave them money to print up their résumés, helped them with their projects, hired baby-sitters for their children so they could finish college, inspired them with gratuitous career advice, and paid the first and last months' rent on a lot of their apartments. In general, he set them up, then sent them on their way.

Once when he was traveling for his own business, he met Sherry, a young woman in her thirties, who was working a convention booth. She happened to mention, as they were chatting, that she'd always wanted to live in his hometown. He gave her his card and casually told her that, if she was "ever in the neighborhood," she ought to stop by.

Months passed, and one afternoon Bill did get a call from Sherry. She said she was in town and wanted to collect on his invitation. Bill invited her over for tea, took her out to dinner, and when they had finished the meal, asked her where she was staying so he could drop her off. Only then did she mention that she'd arrived by Greyhound bus. She'd had a hard year, she told Bill; she didn't have a car, but acting on impulse, she'd decided to move to Bill's hometown and look for a job.

Bill's default instantly kicked into gear. His son had recently gone off to college; he had a spare bedroom. If she liked, he told her, she could stay as a non-paying roommate for a couple of weeks until she found a job and got settled. Sherry moved in. She had trouble finding a job, became discouraged after her first few attempts, and stopped looking. Instead, she scraped along on the unemployment she still had coming in and became a solitaire-playing, television-watching couch slug, "paying for her keep" by washing the dishes and, on occasion, cleaning the house.

Bill was concerned. Maybe he hadn't done enough. Maybe she needed a car to look for a job. He bought her a car. Of course, her unemployment wasn't enough to cover the payments, so he agreed to pay half — at least for a year. Sherry went out once again to look for a job, and once again couldn't find one. By then she had started to help Bill a little with his business, sorting and filing his papers, typing some letters for him. She liked office work, she told him, and said she was considering becoming a paralegal, though of course, she'd have to go back to school to do that.

Naturally, Bill decided to help her. After all, she was trying to get her life together, and by then he also knew that she didn't have much of a family. He paid her tuition, got her a gas card, and allowed her to go on living at his house as she started her first semester.

Several months down this path, Bill met a woman who interested him as a possible mate. She was pretty, cheerful, and buoyant, and he fell for her like a ton of bricks. Soon after they got involved, though, she, too, started leaning on him for support. "Can't you just give me some money for a babysitter?" she'd often ask when they were planning an evening out.

Then Bill suddenly realized that what he always did with women was give, give, give; rescue, rescue, rescue. He cancelled their next date without explanation. A week later he gave Sherry "a one-month notice" on her living space, a two-month notice on the car payments and the gas card, and a final notice on her school tuition. He then went into therapy to find out where he had acquired his default behavior. It turned out that the "helping" had started with his widowed mother. After his father had died, his mother had always tried but never quite succeeded in getting her life together.

In the aftermath of this insight, Bill turned his rescuing behavior into rescuing endangered species. After several years of not dating, he met a woman in the Sierra Club who shared his "rescuing gene." Promising to protect each other from their "dangerous default behavior," they eventually married and have just completed six enjoyable years together.

THE DRINKER

Rob created a crisis when, after his girlfriend threatened to leave him, he responded by hitting her, and as a result, spent a night in jail. He followed that with a drinking binge that landed him, for the sixth time, in rehab.

As he eventually learned there, he couldn't deal with his feelings. Drinking was his default. Realizing he'd never faced anything in his life — his grief, his rage, his discouragement and depression — and that he'd always coped with everything by drinking, he was finally able to stop drinking, commit himself to the AA program, and go to school. In time, he became a rehabilitation counselor.

THE SHOPPER

Paula was a pathological shopper. She shopped every weekend because she was bored, because she was lonely, because she was scared to try to be the songwriter that she'd always wanted to be. She'd go out and buy things, take them home, try them on, install them in her house, and then, recognizing she couldn't really afford them, bring most of them back the next weekend.

In spite of all her returning, she racked up a credit card debt that was slowly grinding her into the ground. When she had a dental emergency that slammed her over her credit card limit, she finally realized the insanity of her ways. She faced her default, drew up a payment plan with her dentist, cut up all her credit cards, and started systematically paying off all her debts. With the time she used to spend shopping, she'd pick away at her piano and work on a song. She has a raft of songs now, almost all her debt is gone, and she recently won first prize at a new songwriters' competition.

Bill, Rob, and Paula each used their crisis as an opportunity to face their defaults, to learn that how they always responded was contributing to the situation. As a result, each of them found deep healing.

RECOGNIZING YOUR DEFAULTS

Defaults come in many shapes and sizes, and it's important to recognize yours. They can be physical, such as eating, smoking, drinking, or getting stoned. They can be emotional, such as always taking the blame, putting everyone else's needs ahead of yours, being the rescuer, always giving too much, blaming everyone else, or always calling for help without actually letting others help you. Your default could be compulsively saving money like a maniac and then being so cheap that you never get a moment's enjoyment out of life, or conversely, it might be overspending in such grandiose and self-indulgent ways that you're always in debt.

Perhaps your default is being a workaholic or indulging in internet madness — endlessly texting, web surfing, and blogging. It might be living in despair, being a cynic, or being an inappropriate optimist (like a loan officer in 2007). Maybe you're always looking and holding out for "the perfect mate," or perhaps you always seem to choose the perfectly wrong person: you're the woman who always dates the complex, fascinating, artistic Bad Boy Lover who hasn't got a cent. The list is endless.

Default behaviors can even be spiritual — being hooked on and endlessly repeating such phrases as "everything's perfect" and "everything happens for a reason" when the *Titanic* is going down or the Dow Jones average is sinking like a stone. Or maybe you meditate six hours a day instead of having the courage to have a conversation with your wife about your teenage son who's just been arrested for selling crystal meth.

The clue is in the "always" quality of your behavior. What is your habitual response to the difficulties of life? Notice how you "always" react; that's where you'll discover your defaults. Until you find and face yours, they will keep you heading for a train wreck.

Living in Defaultville: The Six Life Themes

As I've already mentioned, default behaviors are coping mechanisms, habitual responses that we developed at some point in our lives. In the beginning they were purposeful and meaningful, but how did we start applying them all over the place? It has to do with the fact that we are human psychological beings and that each of us has a particular Life Theme. Although we are spirits, when we arrive on earth, we get born into families — whether our biological families or others. One way or another we arrive in a human psychological context, and so begins each of our life stories.

The components of your story — who your parents and siblings are, how they interact with you, along with the array of other life circumstances you grew up with — all combine to create your Life Theme. Your particular theme is the psychological riddle you are solving in this life.

Everybody has a Life Theme. I do. You do, too. We're not always aware of our themes, or just how they operate in our lives, but like bottom-feeding fish, they are always swimming around in the murky depths of our unconscious, causing us to behave, develop, and react in a particular way.

The tone of your Life Theme may have been chimed at your birth — maybe you were the first of twelve children and your parents had no money. Or it may have been sounded somewhere along the way — perhaps you were doing just fine until your baby brother arrived when you were three. Or perhaps it showed up dramatically when a significant event altered the arc of your story — your father was killed in a car accident driving home one snowy evening after work when you were seven.

These initial chords set up a resonance in our psyches, and as they are compounded, strongly or faintly, throughout our lives through repetitive or additional experiences, our habitual responses to them also become stronger. So it is that the oldest child in the impoverished family of twelve finds himself spending his childhood caring for all the younger children and feeling he never gets the attention he craves. Over time, through the formation of his default behaviors, he finds himself in adult life endlessly scrabbling for money, taking care of the needs of others, and always feeling shortchanged himself. Similarly, the girl who is displaced by her baby brother — the boy her parents wanted all along — may find herself always feeling inferior to or always competing with boys; ultimately, she may compete with the man she marries until he divorces her. And the son of the man who dies on the snowy road and finds himself suddenly "the man of the house" may develop the default behavior of feeling he has to rescue every woman he comes across.

Chords of our initial experience become themes when they are repeated so often that we find ourselves saying or feeling, "Well, that's just the story of my life." This happens when, in response to the original trauma, circumstance, or event, we find ourselves responding with a compensating — or default — behavior. The theme is deepened when we have subsequent experiences that arouse the same feeling tone in us, and that cause us to respond yet again with the adaptive behaviors that we have already developed.

Although each of us has our own unique and nuanced variation, psychological Life Themes generally fall into the following six categories.

NEGLECT

When you have suffered a basic lack of physical, emotional, or spiritual care, your Life Theme is probably *neglect*. Perhaps your parents were too wrapped up in their own problems or circumstances to be there for you — to feed you, talk to you, spend time with you, create a clean or safe environment for you, or teach you how to take care of yourself. Neglect is about being ignored, not being attended to, not being emotionally cared for in the very basic ways that every human being needs and deserves in order to grow and thrive.

If you were neglected, you will have difficulty feeling worthy and treating yourself well, and your defaults may be self-destructive or self-neglectful behaviors such as overeating or overindulging in anything.

ABANDONMENT

If you experienced the painful absence of one or both parents, and didn't have a sense that they were there to provide, protect, or just plain be present for you, your Life Theme is probably *abandonment*. The death or prolonged absence of a parent is a form of abandonment. Parents who leave repeatedly also create a wound of abandonment. Emotional disconnection, deadness, and silence, as well as a refusal to engage, are all forms of emotional abandonment. The denial of your spiritual gifts is also a form of abandonment.

If abandonment is your theme, you are afraid to engage with life or others for fear of losing them again. Or, conversely, because abandonment is familiar, you may repeatedly engage with people who will abandon you once again.

ABUSE

If you endured assault and insult to your physical, emotional, or spiritual being, your Life Theme is probably *abuse*. We usually think of abuse in physical or sexual terms, and those are certainly two of its most devastating forms, but you can also be profoundly abused through emotional insult, nonstop criticism, violating put-downs, verbal competition, or the negation of your spirit. Abuse is attack, the violation of your energy, your physical boundaries, your emotional body, or your soul. Spiritual abuse occurs, for example, when parents refuse to believe that a child has or can have a powerful spiritual gift, such as psychic ability or a special connection to nature; instead of appreciating them, they attack or denigrate these gifts. The term *abuse* refers to the depth of the insult.

If abuse is your theme, you will have difficulty trusting life, and you often put distance between yourself, other people, and experiences — in a variety of ways — to continue to abuse yourself.

REJECTION

When who you are and how you are are not accepted by your parents and, subsequently, by others along your path, *rejection* is probably your theme. It occurs when you are displaced by a favored other, when your parents wish you'd never been born, when they prefer another child to you, or when they blatantly tell you they don't like you.

If rejection is your theme, you find yourself somehow always sitting on the sidelines, not feeling included or a worthy part of your family, group, or community. If you were rejected, you will tend to undervalue yourself, be passive toward opportunities that could give you a sense of your own worth, and attract people and situations that make you feel rejected again. Your default behaviors will center around not being able to take a life-affirming stance on your own behalf.

EMOTIONAL SUFFOCATION

When one or both of your parents were overly involved in your life, used you as a surrogate spouse, relied on you too much, told you all their troubles, made sure that you preferred them to anyone else, opposed your friendships, controlled your movements, wanted to know your every feeling, insisted that they knew, loved, and understood you better than anyone else, or prevented you from establishing allegiances apart from them, *emotional suffocation* is very likely your theme.

If this is your theme, you feel that your emotional body is not your own and is being invaded and appropriated by others, and you have difficulty discovering what you feel, believe, need, and want. Your default behaviors will include not being able to take a stand for yourself, speak up for yourself, or hold your own in circumstances where you are being tested.

DEPRIVATION

When you did not receive the basic modicum of food, clothing, or shelter, *deprivation* is probably your theme. Deprivation is an experience of lack, of not having enough — a complete absence or inadequate supply of time, energy, money, or sustenance. Although similar to neglect, deprivation is about a shortage of what you actually need in order to survive or grow. If, in one or more areas, you have not received enough to allow you to feel that you can make it through your life, you have been deprived.

If deprivation is your theme, you will tend to cope by perpetuating the lack, not trusting that life or the people around you will provide for or share with you. Your default behaviors may be overspending, overextending, excessive generosity — or the opposite, hoarding — so that one way or another, once again there's not enough for you.

Four Steps to Facing Your Defaults

You will notice that none of these are happy themes. Psychological Life Themes are not about your talents, beauty, or intelligence, the number of Facebook friends or Twitter followers you have, or all the great things that are lying in wait for you in life. These good things take care of themselves. They are the gifts, the joys of life. Your Life Theme, on the other hand, is the riddle you must solve, the painful, frequently repeating conundrum that is asking you to understand it and resolve it in this lifetime. That's because each of our lives is a journey of emotional and spiritual evolution that asks us, through the riddle of our themes, to learn how to love ourselves, practice compassion, serve our purpose, and expand our souls.

Defaults are compensating behaviors, things we did to try to make up for what wasn't working right in our childhoods. It's as if, one way or another, we kept saying to our parents, "If I do this, will you love me?" Or to ourselves, "If I distract myself like this, maybe I won't notice the depth of my pain." Because these are unconscious behaviors — something we developed without really being aware we were doing so — we just keep on doing them, whether or not they apply in the current situation. In your present crisis, your soul is asking you to expand the fullness of your humanity. That is, instead of responding the way you did as a suffering child — by using a default behavior — to respond to your pain in a more creative and courageous way.

In one way or another, we are all dealing with these painful emotional wounds. We fill the pain of our hurts with coping behaviors — with defaults. Mommy doesn't have any time for me, so I'll eat. Daddy died, and that's so excruciatingly painful that I'll numb myself with TV, video games, and, as I get older, booze. Nobody around here cares about me anyway, so I might as well go shopping and buy myself a bunch of stuff, then maybe I'll feel better.

The best way to deal with the emotional pain of our Life Themes is, of course, to deal with it directly by going through a process of emotional healing. This generally consists of the following four steps:

1. Recognize that you have a Life Theme which has affected you deeply.

2. Identify the specific way you have been emotionally wounded, and then name your wounds by writing them down or by speaking them to a qualified listener: a priest, an AA sponsor, a therapist, a counselor, or a healer.

3. Notice the way you have tried to address them through the default behaviors you have developed.

4. Go through an emotional healing process, which generally includes feeling your sorrow and anger and then grieving your loss until you come to a place of emotional equilibrium. (This is often best accomplished in the company of a therapist or professional emotional healer, but you can take several steps toward it simply by answering the questions at the end of this chapter.)

Once you have understood your theme and the automatic ways that you've been coping with it, you can consciously choose to face your defaults, change your behavior, and start responding creatively to what life is asking of you. I say "asking of you" because life is inviting you to do a lot more than just default your way to death. It is inviting you to feel your pain, let it go, and then get on with whatever you came here to do.

Just as your Life Theme is unique, so, too, are your gifts, the creativity that you, specifically, have to bring to every life situation, even to this very challenging crisis you're in. You won't get to use these precious gifts, though, and you especially won't have them available to help you through these turbulent times, if you don't first face your defaults.

Living by Your Own Design

My client Alan is a designer who always says: "I don't like to live by other people's designs; I like to live by my own design." When he was thirteen, after his father took off with his cute young secretary, Alan's mother appropriated him as a surrogate husband. Two weeks after his father's disappearance, he had already become his mother's movie date, lawn and garden guy, and personal psychotherapist. Alan was smart enough to know this wasn't good for him, and as soon as he could, he added a bunch of other lawn and garden jobs to his repertoire, sometimes even lying to his mother and telling her that he had extra hours of classes at school, so his mother couldn't always get her hooks in him.

By the time he was eighteen and out of high school, he'd saved enough money to buy a bus ticket to Oregon, where he got a job as a waiter and put himself through college. Although he felt some guilt about leaving his mother, he knew he couldn't serve her forever — a default behavior that might have secured her eternal love but would have cost him his own life.

When he speaks now of living from "my own design," what he means is that he has always preferred to live from a fresh edge, responding to life as it keeps presenting itself. Throughout his life, Alan's been thinking of new solutions: creating furniture out of cardboard boxes when he was still in graduate school; building fabric walls in his apartment, so he could rent out the "extra room"; taking two vacations — one right after another — so he could "get really rested."

Alan's ingenuity, his courage in stepping out of what could have been a lifetime of living by default, has continued to pay off for him. He became one of the first successful designers of corrugated furniture and workspace modules, and he has since gone on to live in a tiny four-hundred-square-foot house, a jewel of artistic construction that gracefully houses all he needs. He also raises his own vegetables and takes a three-month deep-sea fishing vacation every year. He is a man who keeps re-creating himself, a person who is definitely living by his own design.

Unlike Alan, most of us end up living by someone else's design, especially in times of crisis, simply because the default-driven part of ourselves is so ingrained that it keeps us from taking a risk. It takes energy and imagination and guts to keep reinventing yourself, to keep showing up with whatever the moment is asking for. It takes creativity and strength to notice that life is now asking for a completely different response. And it takes courage to discover just what that response might be — swim like hell in the same direction as the sharks (so they don't feel your fear and tag you as prey), sell all your stocks in spite of the fact that your broker keeps telling you to "just hang on," or dig up your driveway and plant an organic garden.

A crisis is always a chance not only to scrape away the film of your defaults but to see that life is inviting you to develop, to move in the direction of your own creative aliveness, to become more of who you are. In this way, pain is the initiator of great change, and crisis is definitely an opportunity. Indeed, it is an unsolicited chance to become more of yourself, more than you ever have been.

Defaults and Self-Sabotage

Facing your defaults is also the only way you'll be able to see how you are cooperating with — and at least in part creating — the very circumstances that are driving you mad. Off-the-charts optimist? What were you thinking when you bought that $500,000 house on a $17,000 salary — and who cares who talked you into it? And you, what were you thinking when you decided to marry the guy who was so drunk on your first date that he couldn't remember your (or probably even his own) name?

There's a beauty in facing your defaults. It's a way of taking yourself by the hand and stepping back — to see what's really been going on — in order to step forward, into the realm of the real. It's about finally seeing that little (or gigantic) blind spot in your behavior, which, without your ever noticing, has been quietly running your life. That awareness is the beginning of change, the doorway to doing something different, the passport to creating a response that actually applies in the current situation, the ticket to a new beginning.

Whatever the nature of the crisis you're in, it isn't just inviting you to change; it is insisting that you do. It's telling you to wake up: wake up to what's really going on here. Wake up to your real self — the good, the bad, and the default — so you can start creating responses that are alive and worthy of this one and only scary, gorgeous, unrepeatable life you've been given.

❧ You and Your Defaults ❧

As we have seen, our defaults are related to our Life Themes, both of which we are ordinarily unaware of. The questions below offer an opportunity to bring both of them into your consciousness and, as a consequence, to make the changes that this new awareness can inspire. Good luck!

- So far as you can tell, what is your predominant Life Theme?

- What are your most prominent default behaviors? That is, what are the behaviors or attitudes you most often use to deal with, escape from, or avoid the painful realities of life? Overeating? Negativity? Passivity? Doing too

much for everyone else? Drugs? Smoking?
TV? Internet madness? Being a phone-aholic?

- When, so far as you can tell, did you develop
your defaults? How old were you? What were
the circumstances?

- How have your defaults contributed to the crisis you are in?

- What would be one step you could take to start
dismantling your default? Cut up all but one
of your credit cards? Throw away your ciga-
rettes? Clean all the junk food out of your cupboards?

- What is one small step you could take in the
direction of a new behavior to cope with life
in a more forthright or creative way? Would it
be to start walking an hour in the morning?
Set up a meeting with a financial advisor? Start
attending AA meetings?

If you want to get through this crisis,
you will have to

Do Something Different

CHAPTER 3

Do Something Different

"We all like to stay on the little crutches that are familiar."

— Jules Zimmer

Different circumstances call on us to be different. To grow or die. To expand or contract. To fly or get lost in the rubble. As our world changes, we must change. When our circumstances are altered, we must alter our responses to them.

There's a purpose to the crisis you're in and part of its purpose is that, through it, in a very profound way, the cosmos is inviting you to have a different experience of life and of yourself. Reality is bumping you up a notch, saying, in effect: you thought life was about "getting and spending," as the poet William Wordsworth once wrote, but it's not. It's about becoming a greater expression of yourself, stepping into alignment with who you truly are, getting on the path that is yours to walk in this life, and connecting with the purpose that is yours, uniquely, to fulfill.

Human life is a journey of evolution. It's not a holding tank, a riff on the status quo, or a meditation on compression and restriction. It is a journey of possibilities, a call to awakening, a path of expansion, emotionally and spiritually. Because this is true, the energy of life itself is constantly teasing, inviting, cajoling us to become more of who we really are; when it meets with continued resistance, it will start urging and insisting.

Since ease and peace are comfortable states, when we're in them, we tend to want to remain there. While they may not be particularly exciting, they're not particularly taxing, either. We can "hang out" in the status quo for a very long time, and since, in fact, we pretty much prefer to, we will likely not be inspired to expand, transform, or evolve in any significant way as long as life is rolling along "in the pink."

The Benefit of Crisis

When a crisis occurs, it's asking not only that we scramble and find some tools to deal with the vexing

48

problems at hand, but also that we grow. Tough times, pain, illness, radically changed circumstances, walls that cave in, rugs that get pulled out from under us, floods that inundate, fires that turn our worlds to heaps of ashes — these "inspire" us to do something different, to become more, better, other than we have been. Indeed, these disasters are all the ways the cosmos has of saying: we've been wanting you to do something different. You didn't get it the first time — or the first hundred times — so, we've provided yet another opportunity, a "discount special" for This Life Only, for you to make the changes your soul has been crying out for.

When you're in the midst of the mayhem, of course, it doesn't feel like a process of expansion. It feels more like the changes you're making are all somehow taking you in the direction of *less* — being less, having less, accepting less, whether it's goodies, status, money, or time. It is actually only by doing something different that you can move yourself through the eye of the storm of your crisis and actually come out with more: more time, tranquility, equanimity, awareness of your purpose, sense of connection, gratitude, peace, hope, love.

Stepping Out of Your Comfort Zone

There are a lot of levels of doing something different. One is attitudinal. Another is emotional. Another is acting in ways you've never acted before. Whichever it is, it's often a natural consequence of facing your defaults. Once you've figured out what you've always been doing that hasn't gotten you anywhere, you can actually contemplate changing your behavior. Doing something different may not always take the form of creating new circumstances or immediate real-world solutions. Often, and more importantly, it can be making changes in the inner landscape of your life — moving from complaint to celebration, from criticism to outrageous praise, from aggression to surrender, from fear, panic, and terror to a loving embrace of life.

This is no small thing. That's because the way you respond to life has a powerful effect on how your life works and feels to you. It has now been scientifically demonstrated that when we operate from the lower emotions like greed, envy, jealousy, fear, and panic, our bodies circulate energy at sluggish, toxicity-producing levels, which don't allow us to grow in consciousness. On the other hand, when we operate from feelings that have a high vibrational charge — emotions such as courage, joy, and compassion — our lives feel blessed and electric. When you live at these higher-vibration emotional frequencies, your consciousness expands and your capacity for love is automatically enlarged. In spite of challenge and crisis, you feel more alive, more at home in the world, more at peace with the stripe of life you are living.

Are you living on a diet of negative thoughts?

Make it a spiritual practice to turn every single one of them around. Is it "another rotten foggy day"? Turn it around by thinking: "It's such a beautiful soft gray day; finally, I can stay inside and get some work done." Do you live by the hackneyed assumption "it'll never happen to me"? Turn it around by thinking: "Wow! Who knows what the universe has in store?!" The minute you make this shift, the entire universe will start to shiver with excitement, and changes you can hardly imagine will start to occur.

That's because when we change the way we talk to ourselves, we change the energy in our bodies (and also the vibrational field around us). I've often said that prayer is a change of attitude in every cell, and we now know that, even on a scientific level, this turns out to be true. When you cry out to the universe with a request for change, you have already, internally, started to create that change by *changing your relationship to the problem.* Simply uttering the request moves the problem from the Can't Be Changed column to the Miracles Can Happen side of the ledger — because you are saying, on a cellular level: I don't believe the status quo is eternal. Life is fluid. This may be a pile of horseshit, but I swear to God, somewhere in here there's a pony.

Imagine a Future You Can't Imagine

Changing your consciousness, and thus your experience of life, begins with an act of courage. No matter how scared you may be in the circumstances that are besetting you now, if you just take a leap into the unknown — whether that's a literal bungee jump across an abyss or saying some words you thought you could never utter — you will find that your reality starts changing. What you did in the past is what brought you to where you are; what you have the courage to do from now on is what will bring a new world to you.

So it is that through one or a series of simple, small acts of courage, you, the TV-addict couch potato, have become you, the heirloom tomato–raising organic gardener. You, the endless naysayer, have decided that no matter what hellish state your exchequer or your romance is in, from now on, you will say to all inquisitors who ask you how you are: "I'm wonderful. Everything's going great" — until, remarkably, a lot of unsolicited opportunities start showing up at your door. You, the emotionally shutdown, straitlaced control freak, decide to put your head in your girlfriend's lap and have a good bawl the day you don't get the job. Then you tell her how scared you are and how small you feel, and for the first time in your life you get the response of tenderness and acceptance that you've always longed for. You, the nose-to-the-grindstone cheapskate, when you get fired, instead of despairing, decide to trust, set out in a sailboat with your sweetheart, and end up writing a travel adventure book. You, the overweight Krispy Kreme addict, decide to run a marathon, and three years later become the living example to your daughter's third-grade class of what a svelte, healthy woman of fifty-two can look like.

Every time you move the furniture (literal or otherwise) in your life, you are creating a new template of your existence in relation to your circumstances. Just because of that movement, just because of the new vibrational energy pulsating in your life, there are suddenly new possibilities. Doing something different will also carry you to hope, because hope always resides in the realm of possibility and change.

A Gift of Aliveness: The Emotional Do-Something-Different

My client Daniel was a professional complainer. He complained about everything in his actually quite comfortable life. He was a successful accountant and had a job at an upscale software firm, but he was always complaining about the long commute, the people who made noise above his apartment, his girlfriend who wanted to spend more time with him, the weather, the smog, his colleagues at work, the bad restaurants near his office, the fact that he could have been earning more had he lived in a different metropolitan area and been affiliated with a larger accounting firm, and his mother, whose chronic illness was the reason he was still living in the town where he grew up.

One summer afternoon last year, Daniel lost his job. No notice. No advance clue whatsoever. Not even a severance package. Just unemployment and gaping questions about his future. Three weeks later, also with almost no warning, his mother died. Then his girl-friend, sensing that despite his various protestations, he was not about to marry her, announced that she'd started dating someone else. In three weeks, he says, his "whole world capsized."

In our work, Daniel realized that his crisis was an invitation to change the way he related to life: "My entire relationship to life was complaint. Without the things I'd imagined would go on forever, I had nothing to complain about — that is, no life. Suddenly I saw that all the things I did have were invisible to me. My job was a blessing, but I couldn't see that. I had a girlfriend who actually wanted to be with me, to get to know me better, but I was afraid of moving into intimacy with her. And my mother, my only real parent, was dying, but I was so busy being upset about where I was living that, basically, I missed knowing her."

Although there were many painful psychological issues underlying his habitual complaining, Daniel made a commitment to be grateful — no matter what. As he went through numerous job interviews in his effort to find employment, he experienced gratitude that he even had interviews to go to and said thank you to each of his prospective employers. Digging deep into his new relationship with life, he wrote his ex-girlfriend a letter of appreciation and told her how much he had valued their time together. They got together briefly, and although she was clear about not wanting to resume their relationship, he felt grateful about the gracious way it had now come to a conclusion.

His response to his crisis was, as he called it, "a victory of consciousness." Indeed, although he is still working through practical issues — he still hasn't found a new job or a new girlfriend, and he is still dealing with the financial aftermath of his mother's death — he considers this journey he has made the real gift of his experience, because unlike before he is truly living in the vivid aliveness of appreciating his life.

The Save Your Own Life Do-Something-Different

Unlike Daniel, whose call to change was thrust upon him, Rochelle decided to change.

Well, not exactly. An extremely successful real estate agent in a high-profile luxe community, Rochelle was a status-seeking, chained-to-her-cell-phone, Porsche-driving, cocaine-snorting young woman in her early thirties. She looked great, had an "awesome" social life, made valuable contributions to her community, and thought of her nonstop drug-fueled existence as simply the kind of life a successful young person like her would lead.

One morning, reeling on her couch after a heavy night of drugging in the bathroom at a party, she found her brain, as she described it, "locked sideways in my skull" and realized that her glamorous life was, in fact, a trip to hell. Suddenly, more than anything, she realized, she wanted peace. Unlike for many "recreational" drug users, this recognition in itself was enough to make Rochelle decide to do something different.

When she finally pulled herself together later that day, she looked in the paper and decided to call "a fly-by-night healer." She didn't expect much, but decided this would be a first step toward moving in a different direction. In the stunningly beautiful way the cosmos shines on our powerful intentions, the "healer" wasn't flaky, but a man who felt her soul's yearning. He helped to set her on a new path.

She soon realized that she could never change her life if she remained in her current circumstances. She handed in her resignation, packed up her dog and a few possessions, and headed for a little town in a nearby state, where step by intricate step she restructured her life — making new friends, taking a new and very humble job as a receptionist at a day spa, joining the Y and swimming every day. She wrote a letter to the editor at the alternate newspaper about her appreciation at living in her new town. To her surprise, she got a call back from the editor, who expressed an interest in her writing and offered her a chance to write a column. She is currently writing a book on change.

Doing something different doesn't necessarily mean dismantling your entire life. For Cheryl, it consisted of taking a few simple actions. Cheryl is a very intelligent young woman who, during high school, had dated the class valedictorian. However, he'd gone off on a scholarship to Harvard and ditched her, and she was brokenhearted. She also wondered why, now that she was in college, nobody seemed to give her any attention and why, so much of the time, she seemed to be alone. With my help, she began to realize that most of her dating time in the past had been spent on pretty unromantic study dates, in which her boyfriend had picked her brain and got her help to write his papers.

I suggested that maybe in the past she'd overvalued her intelligence in the pursuit of human connection and that now she should start doing two new things: First, smile at every person she spoke to, and second, pay a compliment to each person she encountered. At first she was a little put off by what she thought was a "sappy suggestion," but just the same, she decided to try it.

I noticed with delight that, in spite of herself, she smiled at me immediately and thanked me for my suggestion. She said she knew it was going to feel weird, but when I saw her a few weeks later, she told me that she was already having much warmer connections with people. For the first time in her life, she felt "like a woman and not like a brain."

As Cheryl discovered, the minute you start engaging differently with life, life starts engaging differently with you. The cosmos knows your spirit, underwrites your every breath, and quietly celebrates your courage, and it will rush in to support you.

Crisis Is the Thumbtack on the Seat of Your Soul

As you struggle with the components of your current crisis — the empty house, the empty bank account, the lost job, the crippled knee, the devastated heart — you may well find yourself resenting that your altered circumstances require that you do some things you never even considered doing before. Maybe you don't want to start shopping at thrift stores, quit smoking because you just can't afford it anymore, ride a bike, or move in with your parents. It's easy to think of hard times as an insult because they break us out of our patterns. But the truth is that they are brought to us by life, God, the cosmos, the universe — whatever you choose to call it — precisely so we will get off our duffs and break our old patterns. Your crisis is not incidental; *it is* purposeful. And its purpose, precisely, is to get you to do something different and develop in ways it would never occur to you to contemplate, let alone undertake, should you just keep rowing your boat merrily down the stream of your life.

We are creatures whose psychological purpose and spiritual destiny is to keep evolving, to become, in every direction and on every level, more fully ourselves. We are here to get over what ails us, claim our talents, and then use them to assuage the agony and enlarge the beauty of our human existence. If, as a consequence of your Life Theme, the entrenched practice of your defaults, or simply because of the tedium of life itself, you have somehow managed to avoid expanding, the cosmos has sent you this thumbtack as a reminder. Like the old Uncle Sam posters from World War II, the universe is pointing its finger at you and saying: We Want You.

So it is that poverty becomes the mother of invention, accident and loss the matrix of spiritual depth, and frustration, exhaustion, and disgust the royal road to creativity. Instead of decrying the fact that life is requiring that you take some strange new steps, you might as well get with the program and simply bumble forward. If you haven't started bumbling yet, you might ask yourself, first of all, what kind of steps might you take? And, second, where do you imagine or notice these steps might be leading?

Remember, too, that you may not be able to see the final destination after your first few tentative steps. A boat far at sea can end up at either North or South America just because somewhere in the middle of the ocean its captain turned the wheel just the teeniest bit in one direction or another. In the same way, making a small change now will eventually lead you in a significantly different direction. Even if you have to correct your course a number of times, the important thing is to start, to take action. Because your crisis is the hand of the universe telling you that it is definitely time to change course.

I'll Always Have Paris

About twenty years ago when I was exhausted from being on a book tour, rushing to meet a new book deadline, and commuting twice a week to my office in Los Angeles, I was having dinner one Friday evening with one of my colleagues. As we finished the meal, he looked across the table and said, "Well, Daphne, what would you like to do now?" Without skipping a beat, I said half-jokingly, "I'd like to go to Paris for the weekend."

The gentleman in question said half-jokingly in return that, unfortunately, he had to be in New York for a meeting on Monday morning, and that, sadly, he wouldn't be able to participate in my wild hare of an idea.

As I started the hundred-mile drive home, contemplating what might have inspired me to make that outrageous suggestion, it occurred to me that some part of me really did want — and maybe even needed — to go to Paris for the weekend. Apparently, I'd been trying to solicit the support of a relative stranger to help me accomplish something that I myself lacked the full maxilla of courage to do. It was after midnight when I got home, but I took down my suitcase and packed. The next morning, I called my travel agent, went to her office, and picked up my ticket. By two that afternoon I was on a plane.

I'd been to Paris just once before, on a two-day business trip, but I vaguely remembered the arrondissement where I'd stayed. With my little snippets of French, I instructed my taxi driver to take me there. When we came to the small hotel where I thought I remembered staying before, I paid the driver and got out. But alas, there weren't any vacant rooms. Unruffled, I walked around the corner with my suitcase and found another little hotel. With the help of the cranky concierge, I ensconced myself in a room there, and to the accompaniment of café au lait and croissants, I wrote like a fiend for three days before flying back home and returning to work the following Monday.

I've gone to Paris every year since, and in that same room, I've written several books.

Practice, Practice, Practice

Doing something different isn't a one-shot deal. Lasting change doesn't happen overnight; it takes practice. It took me five tries — and five different methods (cold turkey, a quit-smoking book, behavior modification, bribery, and finally a class) — to quit smoking. Meditators don't find peace in their first or even their first hundred hours of sitting. Moving takes a helluva lot of packing, finding a job takes sending out a thousand résumés. Change your practice, and it will become a change you can live by; practice your change, and it will become yours forever.

Just as the journey of a thousand miles begins with a single step, so does the journey of a single step begin with a thousand miles of practice. We often see very accomplished people suddenly spring onto the scene and into fame seemingly "out of nowhere." Usually, though, what we're seeing is the result of traveling a long and winding road: the Beatles, for example, played several years in Germany before achieving fame in Britain and America.

That's why you'll need to remember that doing something different is itself a process. Sometimes you'll be aware of the outcome you're seeking, and sometimes you won't. When I blurted out that I wanted to go to Paris, for example, I just knew that I was weary, in a rut, and needed a change. I had no idea that a single weekend trip would launch me into a lifelong writing program.

The same is true for you. What's an inkling you have right now? A single step you could take tomorrow? Something you've always thought of doing but haven't quite gotten around to?

An overweight baker and restaurateur in my neighborhood decided to begin by "just taking a walk around the block" every day before he opened his restaurant for dinner. That was sixty pounds and two years of walking ago.

A successful entrepreneur I know lost all his money in real estate, so he decided to take a class on the internet, launched a couple of stay-at-home web-based businesses, and now lives half the year in Tahiti. That was four studio apartments, six cut-up credit cards, and seven computer education classes ago.

A veteran stewardess was exhausted from twenty-three years of international travel, so she had a hair-washing sink plumbed into the porch of her new house and started a tiny in-home hair salon. That was one three-month leave without pay, six months of research, and twenty plumber visits ago.

The Global Do-Something-Different

Just as a personal crisis is an invitation to live differently, there is a global crisis afoot that is inviting all of humanity to live differently. Individually and as nations, we have to do something different: in the conduct of our personal lives, and in the choices our communities make about how we live on the planet. We are called, among other things, to live *con amore* — that is, with love — in relationship to the earth we inhabit, the cosmos we are part of.

If we hear the call — the plaintive wail, really — of the tragic, beautiful earth onto which we are born, into whose fields our caskets are laid, into whose oceans our ashes are strewn, we will say to one another and ourselves: "Yes, yes, yes! We will do something different. Yes! We will recycle all our bottles and cans. Yes! We will stop using aerosol bombs so we don't kill off the entire ozone layer. Yes! We will learn to live within our means so we don't bankrupt the entire world economy. Yes! We will learn how to talk to one another, so the entire population doesn't have to get divorced. Yes! We will think long and hard before having children so the world doesn't get so sinkingly overpopulated that the planet will have to flood, burn, overheat, freeze, and rain us out in order to have some breathing room of its own again. Yes! We will plant back our forests and shelter our beautiful snow leopards before they all become extinct, so that with its vast green embrace the earth can reach out and shelter us all again."

When we understand that the global crisis is not a joke, and that without the continual living prayer of our actions, the crisis won't go away, we will change our tune: Yes, yes, yes! We will say. Yes, yes, yes, yes, yes! We will do all these things.

⤳ Doing Something Different and You ⤨

We are creatures of habit and generally prefer the security of the status quo, but doing something different is a way of living creatively. In the midst of crisis, it's a way of taking you to a beautiful place you never dreamed of going. The questions that follow are a little railing for you to hold on to as you're going there.

- As far as you can tell, what is this crisis asking you to do differently? What is the motion or emotion you are being urged to engage in, the new response you're being asked to develop? For example: This business crisis is asking me to value my family and, especially, to spend more time with my children. This financial crunch is asking me to live within my means. This heartbreak is asking me to stop being so emotionally selfish.

- The Name of my crisis is _____.

- The Purpose of my crisis is to get me to _____.

- Next, what are the first steps you could make toward changing your direction, attitude, actions, or choices, which these difficult times are asking of you? To spend more time with family, will you adopt a four-day work week? To save money, will you make a payment schedule for your credit cards and cook dinner at home? To be more open-hearted, will you volunteer to help others who are suffering at a shelter, hospice, or prison? Write five or six subsequent steps that could take you in a very different positive direction.

- What is it that you will say to yourself — what mantra, cheerleading rave, or affirmation will you use — to stay on this path of doing something different? For instance, "My family is more important than an extra hundred dollars a week. If I fail with them, no business success even matters." Or, "No matter what happens, I know I have the resources within myself to solve this." Or, "I'm not sure where I'm going, but I'm sure I'm getting there."

If you want to get through this crisis,
you will have to

Let Go

CHAPTER 4

Let Go

"Everything I've ever let go of has claw marks on it."

— Michael Peake

When your life is falling apart, there's always the impulse to hold on: to him, to her, to it; to the way it was, to how you wanted it to be, to how you want it now. But in order to get through a crisis, you will have to let go of whatever is standing in your way or causing the problem; these are the handcuffs around your ankles, the tin cans tied to your tail. You will have to let go of whatever isn't serving you, whatever you no longer need, whatever keeps you from moving forward, whatever you're so attached to that you can't see where you're going.

You may have to let go of your marriage, your friends, your job, your career, your house, your self-image, the way you deal with things, your past, your dreams of the future. I don't know what you'll have to let go of. That's for you to discover, but I do know that you'll have to let go of something.

Letting go is scary. It's a free fall, an act of surrender. It's releasing ways of being and things you thought were important, and then being okay with the fact that they're gone. Though it can feel like passivity, letting go is in fact a shift in consciousness that's a critical part of how you will solve the problem. It takes courage to look at your life and say, this is a helluva pickle I'm in and I need to lighten my load — my financial load, my emotional load, whatever kind of load it is — so I can deal with the reality at hand.

Just as tears are a doorway to the future, so, too, is letting go. When you let go you take an active role in shaping your life because you are taking responsibility not only for an immediate change but also for whatever comes after. When you consciously decide to let go, whatever ensues doesn't just *happen* to you. You're not just a passive pawn in the plot. Deciding to divorce, selling your house, shredding your journal, quitting your job — when you *choose* to take these

actions, you are actively letting go. You are intention-
ally choosing to move yourself in a new direction.

We're not used to letting go. We're used to hanging on for dear life. We hang on for lots of reasons:
because something is familiar; because the past is a
known commodity and the future is a question mark;
because we lack imagination and can't conceive of a
future better than the past we've had; because blankies
(no matter how ragged and trashed they are) and relationships (no matter how complete they already are or
inappropriate they have become) are a comfort to us.
We hang on because we've been taught that persistence is good and we should never give up. Or we're
simply afraid of the free fall, afraid of coming alive as
ourselves.

Having to let go — of things, of the way it was, of
your notion of what the future will look like — often
creates an identity crisis. We like to live according to
our memories of ourselves, of how we were, of the
way things used to be. Inside us are templates of these
memories, armatures on which layer by plaster layer
we have crafted our identities. We think we still are
who we once thought we were, but changing circumstances can force us to reevaluate. As with the alcoholic bag lady roaming the streets who still thinks of
herself as the prom queen, the college valedictorian
who's suddenly just an average student in law school,
it's hard to let go of an old identity and move on. But

if you don't let go of who and what you once were, you won't be available to become whoever and whatever this crisis is inviting you to become. For instance, without the courage to let go, the small business owner who temporarily drove a cab, the special education teacher who was a waitress for a while, and the young accountant who had to move back in with his parents — might have missed becoming the life coach, the owner of a catering business, and the hospital administrator that they have respectively become. Of course, it's easier to cling to the identity of who we once were than to imagine who we might now become, but, frankly, there isn't any future in it.

Letting go, on the other hand, asks you to believe that somewhere across the Big Tent of Life there will be another trapeze bar that you can take hold of after you've let go of this one. It's an act of terror and freedom, of trust and faith that when you let go, you will find something new, better, different.

But unlike the sidelined CEO, instead of letting go with grace, we're often more like the monkey who reaches into the narrow-mouth jar to grab the coconut inside and then get can't get his hand back out, because he just can't bear to let go of the coconut. Often, it's our desire for more that lies at the root of a crisis, and we have to let go of this desire. The happy shopper can't come home with every bargain at the mall. The refugee can't walk out of town with the kitchen stove on his back. Every form of freedom has a price. You can't have everything you've already got and everything you haven't had yet. The living room isn't big enough for the old couch and the new couch both at once. You gotta let go; you gotta take your pick.

Letting go frees up your energy and your attention. In the open field of surrender lie the seeds of new possibilities. Sometimes the content of the new possibility is nothing — you let go and are left with absence, a vacancy. This, in itself, can be a relief: the lightness of being you feel when you've finally dropped those extra fifty pounds, the silken tranquility in the house when you finally ditch your screaming husband.

Letting go means not hoping "things will change," not bargaining or making deals — I'll let go *if;* I'll let go *when.* It's not storing the freeze-dried body of your friendship (or your marriage or your job) in cryonic suspension. It's acknowledging that this piece of your life, this relationship, this way of doing things has served its purpose and so it is time to let go of it completely.

In the less is the more. In the emptiness there is room for so much.

Why Do I Have to Let Go?

When Carlton called me in anguish, his wife of fourteen years had just asked for a separation. When he thought about the past ten years, he could see that he hadn't responded to many of his wife's requests for change. Suddenly he realized that she'd been serious about all the things that she'd been asking for, and he wanted to come and talk with me to see if he could "fix it."

By the time he arrived at my office, it was just beginning to dawn on him that maybe his wife was really asking for a divorce, that maybe his marriage was over. He was shocked, enraged, and terrified as he stumbled into this recognition. In the midst of tears and anger, his agonized question to me was: "But why should I let go?"

Carlton speaks for a lot of us. Why should we let go? Of the woman who's already left you? Of your dream house? Of your anger? Or your greed? Or your need for control? Or your kids — who just turned twenty-six and twenty-nine?

We need to let go because whatever we're holding on to is keeping us attached to the problem. Hanging on is fear; letting go is hope. Holding on is believing that's there's only a past; letting go is knowing that there's a future. In letting go, we surrender the weight of our burdens and find the lightness of being with which to begin once again. We open a door for the intervention of the divine.

In our spiritual depths, we all have a profound sense of the inappropriateness of hanging on to stages of life and ways of being that no longer serve us. We know they're no longer a part of our essence, and yet most of the time, it's very hard to move away from them.

One of the great gifts of crisis, therefore, is that it calls us to this awareness. It insists that we examine our excesses; it invites us back into alignment with the highest and best in ourselves. We feel hope when we are in alignment because we know that we are in the true condition of freedom to fulfill our purpose and find deep meaning in our lives.

New lands await, freedom abounds. Opportunities hide like rain in the clouds waiting for the moment to reveal themselves. The white canvas, crying out for paint, is alive with possibility. The freed man is free to fall in love again; the freed woman to claim her strength, find her true work, begin again at a deeper and more satisfying level.

I've worked with hundreds of people, shepherding them through the endings of their relationships. No matter how grueling the process is in the moment — and it always is — I've never found a single person who said afterward that they wished they could have that relationship back. That's because as human beings we are evolutionary animals. There is a push, a draw in us to move toward and become that which we haven't been yet — more, better, wiser, more deeply loved, more deeply loving.

We are creatures of movement, souls on a journey. This is a one-directional enterprise, and the direction we are moving is forward. There's no other direction, like it or not. Even sideways and backward will eventually carry you forward, if you'll just let go of what's dragging you down. If you don't, you will be frozen, paralyzed, stranded.

Snakes shed their skins, butterflies vacate their cocoons, chameleons drop their tails. It's what you let go of, not what you hang on to, that will bring you to grace and tranquility in the end.

Your Heart Will Lead the Way

When I met my friend Matt, he was thirty-three years old. After getting his MBA, he had launched a successful business career right out of graduate school. Rising through the ranks, he became a manager at twenty-seven. At twenty-eight, working ten-hour days, commuting an hour and a half each way to work, he had his first heart attack. Matt was shocked and devastated — his father had died of a heart attack at fifty-six. Lying in his hospital bed, Matt was encouraged by his CEO to "just take six months off and then you'll be good as new."

Matt decided to take his boss's advice. He sublet his apartment and bought a van. He drove up and down the California coast and camped on the beach for several months, walking along the shore each morning and contemplating his brush with death. The more he thought about it, the more insane it seemed to go back to work. If his job had almost killed him, what was the point of going back? As his healing sabbatical continued, he began to get the sense that he should let go of it all: the job, the commute, the six-figure salary, the three-piece suits, the two-bedroom apartment. After he returned from his trip, he told his boss he wasn't coming back. His boss told him he was crazy, just disoriented by his time away, and he offered Matt a raise, a third as much more income. "You're the best man we've ever had," he said. "You could be the next CEO."

Matt went for a drive in his van and, he admits, wavered for a minute: Should he throw away "all that success" and a "golden future" for...he didn't know what? But the sense he'd had when he was traveling — that he should "let go of it all" — stayed strong with him, and a few days later he went back to work and handed in his resignation.

He lived modestly on his severance pay for the next several months. As he traveled, he gradually changed his eating habits, and took yoga classes in the various towns he passed through. As he went through his own healing process, he gained a new sense of well-being — the first, he realized, that he'd ever had. He realized, too, that his health was really his most important asset. In one of the towns where he stopped, there was a yoga teacher training center. He offered to work in the kitchen if, in exchange for his services, he could go through their teacher training program.

That was eight years ago. Matt is now a certified yoga teacher and successful nutritional consultant. By letting go of everything, he found his true work. Or, as he says lightheartedly, "My heart attack led me to my 'path with a heart.'"

To Let Go You Have to Practice Letting Go

Emily leads a woman's group, and recently she encouraged a conversation about what each person needed to let go of. A number of women had recently gone through some very hard times. One, whose husband had just lost his job, said she needed to let go of nagging. She realized she was so scared about his unemployment that, rather than supporting him, she'd become an insufferable nag.

To train herself to stop, she put a rubber band on her wrist, and each time she started to nag, she would ping herself and shut up. In several weeks she realized that, with only the rarest exception, she had let go of nagging.

Another woman said she wanted to give up her need for control. She'd lost her job, her dog had just died, and she'd just been given a six-week notice that she had to vacate her apartment. She said that her usual way of handling things was to grip tighter and tighter. This time, however, she realized that her circumstances were inviting her to surrender. She decided that, rather than using all her usual control techniques, she'd start meditating every day. Gradually, she began to feel a new sense of equanimity. Within weeks, both a new job and a new apartment showed up for her, "almost by magic."

LETTING GO OF A MARRIAGE

A woman I know told me that three weeks after she married she realized that her marriage was a terrible mistake. She knew she ought to run, not walk, to get out of it. Yet, it took her five years before she had the courage to initiate marriage counseling, which lasted another four arduous years. During those years, she admitted, whenever the counselor suggested that maybe her marriage was over, she would sabotage her escape by leaving that counselor and looking for one who would tell her that she should keep on hanging on, that maybe they could make it work — all because she was so scared of letting go.

She practically had a nervous breakdown when, exhausted by her own shenanigans, she finally let go and ended her marriage. Now, six years later, clear, free, and in possession of herself, she can't imagine what she could have been thinking.

LETTING GO OF A FRIENDSHIP

Laura and Sarah had been best friends for years. They met in college, and their friendship continued after college, through Laura's marriage and Sarah's string of boyfriends, and then through the hectic years when Laura had two children and subsequently got divorced and when Sarah, by then a successful career woman, adopted an infant from Vietnam.

Then, suddenly, the dynamic of their relationship changed. When Laura had been needy and desperate while going through her divorce, they'd been especially close; but when Laura recovered and launched into her new life, Sarah no longer seemed to want to spend any time with her. She was always "busy with her new baby" and often snippy and short when Laura called. When Laura came to talk to me about it, she was devastated by this apparent cooling in their friendship. It seemed as if Sarah had really only liked her when she was "a case," and now that she was "better," Sarah no longer wanted Laura in her life.

Laura had been abandoned by her own mother when she was a little girl, and so Sarah's rejection created an excruciating emotional crisis for her. After months of chilly treatment, despite her many endeavors to connect, Laura decided that, out of love and respect for herself, it was time to let go of the friendship. Her first impulse was to write a snippy letter, telling Sarah how mad and sad she was about the treatment she'd been receiving, then to explain how fabulous and changed she was so Sarah would acknowledge and celebrate her growth.

As she worked on the letter, however, she realized that, rather than letting go, she was actually holding on — to the way it once had been, to the way she wanted it to be. It took several drafts — and a lot of tears — before she was able to write a simple letter of release and farewell. By the time she had gone through this painful and painstaking process, though, she was at peace. When I saw her recently, she mentioned that she was cultivating two new friendships with mothers of her children's friends at school.

THE ULTIMATE LETTING GO

Over the years, from time to time, I've taught workshops on coming to terms with one's own death. The process follows a path of celebrating all that you are and all that you have in this life, and then moves through various stages of letting go. This includes imagining the loss of various physical capacities, your familiar circumstances, your pets and kindred people, your friends, and finally your body and life itself.

Along the way in this process, people feel a profound sense of connection to all that their lives have contained — their houses, beautiful things, rich experiences, health and beauty. As people contemplate the loss of each of these, there are always a great many tears.

What is remarkable, however, is how free and whole people always feel at the end. Although at the moment of letting go there is always a pinch of pain, there is also always, when it's completed, a deep sense of peace and freedom. In fact, in one form or another, to a person, they all say that they feel profoundly liberated, reborn.

Of course, they know they aren't really dying. They know they'll go back to their houses and families once the "death" weekend is over. But the sense of peace and relief they express is always far deeper than just a spurious temporary reprieve. For a moment, they've experienced being liberated from all the things that they're ordinarily engaged with, everything that distracts them and bogs them down. In the space that is cleared, they come in contact with what is eternal and unchanging inside them, what remains after all has been said and done, grasped at and surrendered in this life.

By letting go of everything, they have come into the presence of what will always remain.

PRACTICE, PRACTICE, PRACTICE

How do you let go? Any way you can. Get help — hire the men with the truck to haul your junk away. Trick yourself. Find an ally. Hold hands when you leap from the burning building. Pray for grace. Cry. Practice until you get good at it. Give things away. Throw things away. Sell everything you can. This is all just a show, anyway. We're on our way to somewhere else.

So why be bogged down with fourteen irrelevant people, two tons of useless junk, and a brain full of worry? When, really, you're just practicing to be part of an intergalactic lightstream of Love.

Don't hang on. It's hard to fly with bags of concrete tied to your feet. Let go. Let go. Let go.

⤳ Letting Go and You ⤳

Letting go is an act of surrender, and it's very different from what we're usually taught to do, which is to control, fight, and hang on. I hope that looking at letting go from a new point of view will encourage you to let go and that the examples of people whose surrender has brought them peace, growth, and surprising new opportunities will inspire you as you answer the following questions.

- What are the tin cans on your tail? What are you holding on to that is impeding your freedom as you endeavor to move through this crisis? Debilitating friendships? Unproductive work relationships? A lousy marriage? Hopelessness? Despair? A standard of living you can't afford?

- Pick one area and write one intention that you are committed to fulfilling in the next month. Try to make it something that represents a significant letting go, something that will create new space for new possibilities. Write a farewell letter to the friend you need to let go of. Donate all the clothes you no longer wear to a local charity. Sell the car whose payments you can't meet.

- What do you want to show up in place of what you've let go of? For example: an inspiring job. Breathing room. Emotional balance. A new sweetheart. Stating the new thing you want not only makes letting go much easier but also hastens its arrival. The universe, seeing where you are headed, will support you in getting there.

- We don't often think about our own deaths, but imagine for a moment saying good-bye to the whole of your life. After you do this, ask yourself: If I were dying now, what would be the one thing, person, or way of being I would wish I had already let go of? Your house? A certain relationship you've been hanging on to? Possessions that don't serve you? A fantasy of what your life should be like? The job you're scared to leave? Can you find in your heart a new willingness to let go of it now? What step could you take today toward that letting go? What is the freedom you imagine that, afterward, you might feel?

If you want to get through this crisis,
you will have to

*Remember Who
You've Always Been*

CHAPTER 5

Remember Who You've Always Been

"He knows not his own strength that has not met adversity."

— Cesare Pavese

I n the midst of the current frazzling fray, it's probably easy to feel as if somehow everything's your fault — not because it is, of course, but simply because you're overwhelmed. You feel as if you ought to have the stamina, the resources, the savvy, or the moxie to get yourself out of or through all this — whatever your particular "this" is — and you don't. You feel as if you should have been able to prevent the crisis from happening in the first place — but you didn't. You may feel utterly hopeless, helpless, and defeated as all hell breaks loose in your life, like you have nothing to work with, nothing to count on right now. You may wake up in the morning (or at three in the morning) feeling stripped of everything you ever were, every talent and strength you ever had.

But that's simply not true. When the tectonic plates of the world are shifting beneath your feet, it *is* hard to remember that there's a continuous thread of genius, of power, of responsiveness that runs through your life, that, since the beginning, you've had certain qualities to bring to the task at hand — no matter how fraught it may be with challenge and frustration.

Who you are now is who you've always been. You didn't wake up today as somebody else. You are a single, talented, rare, unrepeatable human being. There is something at your core that's unique to you, that always has been and always will be. This is the throughline of your personal essence, the chiming chord of your unique existence. It has carried you through every day of the year, every year of your life, and it is what will sustain you now. The *you* who has always been you has been preparing for this moment. The power that is in you will rise to this occasion. You are equal to it with your gifts.

In hard times, especially, we tend to forget this. I've been flabbergasted, over the many years I've worked with people, by how often they seem to feel that the person they are now is a completely different person from the one they were as a child. It's as if they think Person A, the adult, is completely distinct and separate from Person C, the child. And that, as a consequence, none of the talents, responses, and ingenuity of that child — as well as none of the sorrows, difficulties, and challenges — still belong to them.

This isn't the case, of course. Because just as your spinal cord runs all the way through your spine, collecting all your snowy white vertebrae together into a single beautiful curved line, there is a through-line of giftedness, a unique and powerful way of responding, that runs throughout your life. Certain things that were true of you at age seven, fourteen, and twenty-one are still true, no matter how much life may be rocking and rolling around you.

Just as a zebra can never become a giraffe, in an essential way you always remain who you always were. And although you may go through a number of dramatic changes in your lifetime — move from one city to another, quit smoking, get sober, get married after years of being an independent cuss of a single person (or, perhaps, get divorced after a thirty-year marriage) — there's a distinctive chord of responsiveness to who you are. It runs through your life like the melodic theme in a symphony, and no matter how radically your circumstances change, its singular melody can still be heard.

This chord that runs through you is what I call your Signature Strength. It is the unique stronghold of your personal power. How you have always used it is one of the things that uniquely defines you, and in times of crisis, it is what will carry you through.

On an emotional level, your Signature Strength is made of your talents and the positive adaptive mechanisms through which you respond creatively to life. Unlike defaults, which are frequently unconscious and often have a self-destructive component, your Signature Strength is the power you bring to solving the riddles of life. It is through using our strengths over time that each of us becomes more and more highly developed as the unique individuals we are. All of our life experiences, especially the difficult ones, are given to us so that, experience by experience, we can further define and refine ourselves. This is the life journey of our personalities.

But on a spiritual level, too, our difficulties have meaning. We are asked to go through them so that our souls can expand their capacity to love. This is the essence of spiritual growth. Our souls, the divine eternal essence in each of us, have arranged exactly the experiences that will cause us to challenge our prejudices, open our hearts, and expand the reach of our compassion.

Your Signature Strength

I ran into my friend Phillip recently, and he started telling me about all the financial hits he's taken in the past couple of years — plummeting stocks and real estate values, a business that's no longer relevant. "But I know I'll be fine," he said, after listing off hundreds of thousands of dollars in losses. "I'm a survivor."

He reminded me that when he was a kid, his father took off, abandoning the family. Afterward, he, his mom, and his brother lived at times in their car, in vans, and sometimes in tents. Despite these rough beginnings, he went on to become a very successful businessman, as did his brother. In fact, together they bought their mom a new house. Now, rough times are upon him again. He isn't happy about it, but he isn't wiped out either. As he repeated again before we parted, "I'm a survivor. I know I'll get through this." He was reminding himself of his capacity to endure, the Signature Strength that's always carried him through.

Your own Signature Strength is a habit of mind or conviction, a steadfast or extraordinary talent, a way of looking at things or dealing with them, which, no matter what your circumstances, will carry you through. It may be endurance, the capacity to hold on to the mast when the boat is threatening to capsize in high seas. Or it could be the ability to analyze things, to be thrifty no matter what your circumstances, to look at life from an upside-down or inside-out point of view that somersaults you into creating exciting solutions. Maybe your strength is the ability to organize, to sequence things so you always do them in just the "right" order, or your focus is such that you never miss the boat because of daydreaming or not paying attention. You may have an exceptional ability to make friends, to network, to speak in a way that touches people deeply or inspires them to come to your aid or the aid of the cause you represent. Your Signature Strength could be the capacity to see core truths: in a piece of writing, a personality, a circumstance, a family squabble, an economic maelstrom, a community crisis. It might be an instinctual gift for knowing how money works, a genius for investing whether the market is up or down. Or it could be the ability to read energy, to empathize, to talk to animals or birds, to nurture children, to draw or dance, to make people laugh, to intuit spatial relations, to design rooms.

Whatever your particular strength, it is crucial that you become aware of it and consciously connect with it now. For no matter what your circumstances — graced and blessed or troubled and challenged — it is a crucial capacity for navigating your way through life. It's always been there. In some sense you were born with it already layered into your tissues the day you arrived. Time and life have developed it and shown you its true colors, and it's what you can count on now.

The precise name and functioning of your Signature Strength may elude you. It may be so intrinsic to how you've always responded to life that you may not even be aware of it. Or maybe you've always recognized it as the one capacity that you could always count on. You may look at the list above and find several strengths that apply. That's because life is generous, and we all have more than a single stick with which to build a fire. But somewhere inside yourself you already know — even if you haven't quite brought it up to consciousness yet — the one main gift that, above all others, is, and always has been, yours.

The trouble is, when life is falling apart, we often can't quite remember who we are and what we've got to bring to the table. Instead of being able to say, like my friend Phillip, "I'm a survivor; I'll make it through even if I have to shine shoes," you can get all weak-kneed and despairing and feel like a butterfly in a typhoon — desperate, pitiful, and unequipped. That's why connecting to your Signature Strength is so important. When you remember your most precious resource, you can have hope! Instead of feeling that your circumstances are bigger than you are, you suddenly realize that, in fact, they are calling out the best in you.

Your Signature Strength Is a Path of Joy

When Steve lost his job in the sock factory, he came home the day he was let go and said it felt like a death. He didn't know how he'd ever get over it. He applied for unemployment and fell into a depression. After a couple of weeks he wrote up a résumé. It was all he could do to write it. It was all he could do to check the internet and send out five résumés a day. By the time he'd sent out a hundred résumés and gotten no response, he was really depressed.

In the middle of his depression and his résumé-sending blitz, he picked up his guitar one morning. He'd played guitar as a teenager. In fact, he'd always wanted to be a guitar player, but life — an early marriage, two kids, the little house in the suburbs — had deferred his teenage dream. Steve noticed that playing made him feel a little better. Not so desperate. He experienced some hope — a little joy even — for the couple of hours each morning when he was playing his guitar.

He remembered some songs he'd written and dug them up. He started practicing. When a friend of his teenage daughter said she wanted some entertainment for her birthday party, Steve's daughter, on a whim, suggested her dad. He sang at the party. Everybody loved it. Soon more of his daughter's friends asked him to sing at their parties. They started paying him, and he started charging. He got a gig at a local restaurant for a little paycheck and tips.

In the two years since, Steve has landed another part-time job and continues to play guitar gigs. He and his wife have cut down on things. Life doesn't look the way it used to. The kids help out by getting jobs after school, and they are going to have to help pay for their college. There aren't as many trips to the mall. But

Steve is happier. His wife is happier. Their lives are happier. Through the backroads and bayous of drastically changed circumstances, he's gotten around to doing what he always wanted to do. Making music was always his Signature Strength.

Don't Give Up!

When times are really terrible, people often have thoughts of throwing in the towel and giving up. Indeed, you may feel so depressed that it seems as if there's no way through. The newspaper keeps bringing us strings of stories about people who have decided to take the final irreversible step — the financier in New York who shot himself in his apartment, the mother and father of five in Southern California who agreed to exterminate themselves and their children as their way of coping with crisis. But unless the cosmos itself has decided to carry you off, it's not time to be done, not time to throw in the towel or the sponge or whatever you feel like throwing in, whether with a loud banshee scream or a pitiful whimper.

Instead, it is time to come once again to the altar of your competence, to claim the riches in yourself, to live the power of who you are, of who you've always been. It's time to tease out the thread your soul has woven through your life. Crisis is a challenge to express your strengths at their highest arc, which is when you also are at your most beautiful.

Your Path Is Walking You,
Even When You're Not Walking It

A few years ago I was in a spiritual crisis. I'd basically taken my life apart — sold my house, sold my car, and taken a pause in order to write the poetry and fiction I'd always told myself I wanted to write. During my sabbatical, I did a lot of that writing while I traveled — in cafés, on trains and planes, in friends' and strangers' houses — but it didn't seem to be coming together, to be getting finished, to amount to anything.

In the middle of this free-form time-out, I'd moved to a town where I knew almost no one, the weather was awful, and I wasn't too crazy about the apartment I'd ended up in — even though it was in a building regarded as an architectural treasure in a beautiful old neighborhood.

I remember walking my trash out to the back alley one afternoon, looking at the dumpster overflowing with other people's beer cans, wine bottles, pizza boxes, appliance boxes, newspapers, *TV Guides*, plastic bags, yard clippings, weeds, macaroni and cheese, coffee grounds, and orange rinds — the quintessential American Garbage Aroma crowding my nostrils — and wondering what the hell I was doing there. What could I have been thinking that I'd completely dismantled my life to float across continents wielding my pen?

Suddenly my life seemed stupid, foolish, crazy. I felt ungrounded, as if even the basement had been pulled out from under me, but it wasn't even all these circumstances in themselves that felt so hard. It was the fact that I'd created them in order to write, and that my writing didn't seem to be adding up to anything.

It was Good Friday, I remember. I went inside, lay down on the couch, and had a good cry. I felt as if I'd somehow foolishly, self-indulgently gotten on the wrong track. It was an ego trip, a mistake, a two-year faux pas. I'd probably gone through it all just to realize that writing wasn't my path. I thought about all the reasons why writing couldn't be, shouldn't be. My father, an English professor, had died before ever reading a word I'd written; my mother, ditto. I had a good yowl about that. I thought about the creative writing teacher at the university who systematically eviscerated the talent of every one of his students — me included — with his brutal criticisms. I remembered wondering at the time how his own children had managed to survive his brutal tongue. (Ironically, one of them, brilliant and still virtually unable to construct a paragraph, years later became one of my clients.) I thought of another writing teacher who, after begging to see my poems, lost all of them. I thought of my poems. The hundreds of rejection slips. The manuscripts growing moss in my closets.

Surrender. Let go, I said to myself. Maybe writing isn't your path.

I felt pretty good after all that, and since I was driving up to my daughter's house the following day, I decided to pack. The next morning I loaded the car and started up the road. I put on one of my favorite CDs and played and replayed a couple of my favorite cuts, like a chant, a mesmerizing mantra. It was a beautiful day and I felt great. Liberated. Freed. Enough of all that. I was done with writing. I'd give my notice on the apartment, move back to California, and reconstruct my life.

It was twilight by the time I arrived at my daughter's house. She'd left a note saying that she'd be back in an hour. I brought my luggage up to my room and got squared away; then I came back down to the kitchen to make myself a cup of tea. Above her antique stove was a newspaper clipping about a recent sociological study. "Whatever most people end up being when they grow up," it said, "it is very likely something they liked to do when they were six or seven."

Bingo! Suddenly I was seven again, lying on the long cement driveway of my childhood home in Michigan. It was summer; I was looking up at the clouds and hearing the sounds of beautiful words as they came fluttering through my mind. Half an hour later, I walked in the house and told my mother that when I grew up, I wanted to be a poet. A few days later, my mother gave me a black-and-white-speckled notebook in which to write all my poems. Thinking about that notebook — which I still have — a few little tears started to tremble their way down my cheeks.

I thought about how when I was thirteen I'd won the all-city poetry contest, how I won poetry contests again in college and in graduate school, and still later in the newspaper of the small town where I lived for several years. I realized that in spite of my doubts, in spite of my tears, I had always been on my path. Writing — my love of language, my fascination with the sound of words, the meaning, inspiration, and depth that can be conveyed through them, my desire to reveal emotions through them, the physical act of writing itself — had always been with me, in good times and bad, as play, as work, as the bridge for making my way across life's abysses. My Signature Strength, even when I had doubts to the point of wanting to give it all up, even when I wasn't paying attention, had been there always, over, under, around, and through everything, carrying me along.

I made my tea, and I was still blowing my nose a few minutes later when my daughter walked into the kitchen. "Are you alright, Mom?" she asked. "Yes," I said, giving her a hug. "I'm fine."

The next day, I sat in Molly's garden and wrote a

couple of memoir pieces, one each about my father and my mother. From time to time, I perform them, and people are always moved when I do.

In Each of Us

As I was writing one night, I went for a walk on the beach. It was beautiful twilight, the sun just setting, the clouds going pink in the sky. I walked down the road from the park to the beach, and then along the beach heading south. As I did, I came upon a seagull standing on a single leg, who was also out having an evening walk, his single foot tiptoeing shyly into the water. Amazingly, majestically, he was balancing his curved and lovely body, a body the size of a football, on a leg the size of a knitting needle.

I was touched by the sight. How had he lost his leg? At birth? To the jaws of a shark? The bill of a seagull? The teeth of a dog? What I wondered even more was what kept him going. What Signature Strength had allowed him — no, not allowed, but directed, insisted, commanded him despite his terrible loss — to come out tonight for a walk. Was it a gift for balance? Love of the sunset? The inspiration of challenge? Determination? A love of the water? The will to keep traveling with his mates?

I'll never know, of course, and it doesn't matter. The gull had done his work, inspiring me, reminding me that in each of us there is a unique, powerful impulse, a way we always engage with life that is utterly consistent with who we are at the core.

What is the leg you can stand on when you've lost your other leg?

⚛ Remembering Who You've Always Been ⚛

A surprising thing about your Signature Strength is that it's been a part of you for so long that you can scarcely see it. People all around you have always noticed your talents (whether they've bothered to tell you or not), and you've been using them all your life. But even so, you may have never paused to really take account of them. One of the gifts of the crisis you're in is that it's a chance to really claim these riches that are yours. I hope the following questions will help.

- What, if you think about it quickly right now, is your Signature Strength? If it doesn't come immediately to mind, ask yourself what you liked to do when you were a child of six or seven.

- How has this Signature Strength of yours, this talent, attitude, or gift, served to carry you through your life?

- If you tweaked it, recognized it, or valued it more, how could you use your Signature Strength to carry you through this current crisis?

If you want to get through this crisis,
you will have to

Persist

CHAPTER 6

Persist

"Nothing in this world can take the place of persistence. Talent will not; nothing is more common than unsuccessful people with talent. Genius will not; unrewarded genius is almost a proverb. Education will not; the world is full of educated derelicts. Persistence and determination alone are omnipotent. The slogan 'press on' has solved and always will solve the problems of the human race."

— Calvin Coolidge

Persistence is the spiritual grace that allows you to continue to act with optimism even when you feel trapped in the pit of hell. It is the steadfast, continual, simple — and at times excruciatingly difficult — practice of trudging forward until the difficult present you're scared will go on forever is replaced by a future that has a new color scheme.

Persistence isn't fluffy or humorous (although it can benefit from frequent infusions of humor) or stupidly optimistic. Persistence is intention embodied, repeatedly, in action. It's seeing something through, even when it seems like you're not getting anywhere, because inside you know a solution is coming toward you that is different from the present, and that when it arrives it will hold a cornucopia of new possibilities.

Somewhere in the distance, your future is holding out its arms to meet you, ready to bring you whatever you've had the courage to ask for. It is already holding in trust whatever you have the courage to keep steadfastly moving toward. It wants to join hands with you to create the next chapter of your life, but it won't — it can't — if you stay riveted to the same spot, whining and complaining, passive, fearful, and resentful. That's because the future always comes toward us in exactly the spirit in which we approach it — hands and heart open, or souls withered in defeat.

When you decide to persist, it's not because you're an idiot, not because you don't know from the inside or from looking around just how dire your current circumstances are. It's because in the face of perhaps thousands of reasons to be discouraged, you choose to be bold, to carry on, to keep on duking it out, no matter how grizzly, tedious, intractable, or seemingly hopeless the present situation may seem. The power of persistence is required especially when we're dealing with intense, emotionally devastating circumstances or bunches of hugely difficult things that have stacked up all at once. When you're facing a diagnosis of Graves' disease, a taxi accident, and the imminent death of your sister, *and* your boyfriend has just moved to Japan, you will definitely need to call on persistence.

Sometimes the persistence that can transform a whole life lasts just a few minutes — as in the case of the soldier who slings his buddy's bleeding body up over his shoulder and lugs him across the desert until he can deliver him to the medivac copter. Sometimes it is a life's work, an Erin Brockovich–like crusade of endlessly knocking on doors, talking to strangers, gathering evidence, and poring through mountains of papers until, finally, you uncover the facts that can change everything.

Persistence is guts. Stick-to-itiveness. Determination. The willingness to repeat and repeat and repeat until you've achieved the desired effect. Persistence says: Don't give up!

In this sense, persistence is visionary. Expectant. A sacred journey resplendent with hope. When you persist you know, on a visceral level, that you are enacting your part in the invisible contract between you and the cosmos. Instead of feeling powerless, you feel alive. Instead of feeling hopeless, you have a sense that you're on the path to somewhere. Instead of feeling like a victim, you feel like a person of action; in your deep self you know that this choice for action will one day be rewarded with a response.

Persistence is the journey of effectiveness that allows you to hope. It is the energy that wants to get things done, to assist you in moving from crisis to solution. Persistence can take you from debt to solvency, from heartbreak to true love, from sickness to health, from foreclosure to having a home. Emotionally, it can take you from fear to joy; spiritually, it can deliver you from despair to peace. So persist, be steadfast in your undertaking, for only the path consistently traveled can deliver you to the outcome you long for.

Whatever your battle, it's never easy. The monsters never just slink back into the woods with their tails between their legs. They will fight you for every breath. There is a battle in this universe for every inch of light, and only those who persist will rise to behold the astonishing light of the sunrise.

Persistence Wins the Day

I have a friend, a divorced bachelor named Wally. I hadn't seen him for about four years, when a business matter caused me to ring him up one afternoon recently. Answering Wally's phone when I called was one of the sweetest female voices I'd heard in a very long time.

When Wally came to the phone, I remarked on the lovely voice of, I assumed, his new secretary. He told me that the woman was, in fact, his wife, and that he hoped we could handle our business quickly, as they were packing for a trip to Europe. I congratulated him on both matters, and then Wally said, "Well, since you're so happy for me, I'll have to tell you the story of how we hooked up."

Unbeknownst to me, in the ten years following his divorce, Wally had basically given up on dating. His ex-wife had an ongoing health issue and, at the time of their divorce, had sued him for lifetime health care that amounted to more than half of his annual salary. He'd been so stretched financially and so in the dumps emotionally that he'd decided he would never marry again. Eventually, though, he missed the joy of a companion, and he decided to make a concerted effort to find the woman with whom he'd be happy to spend the rest of his life.

He chose the personal ads in his hometown paper as his search engine because, he said, he thought they were somehow "more personal" than the avalanches of information offered on internet dating sites. In his ad, he talked about what he thought he had to bring to the table of love and the qualities he'd like to find in a mate. Then he decided that he'd at least have coffee with each of his respondents.

He told me that he worked his way slowly, steadfastly, arduously, *persistently* through the seventy-seven respondents to his ad — waitresses, lawyers, single mothers, a grandmother or two (Wally's sixty-four), one open-minded lesbian who thought she might be ready for a change, a lap dancer, a choreographer, a jazz dance teacher, one Vietnamese manicurist, two police-women, one bus driver, one bartender, four secretaries, two psychologists, two painters, and one pilot — before he heard an "angelic" voice reaching out to his spirit, the same one that had answered the phone when I called.

Wally had searched for two and a half years before he finally connected with Jen, who'd answered more than thirty ads herself. He said that along the way he'd learned a lot about women, about their kindness and their needs, about their loneliness. He told me that he was a wiser, kinder, and far more grateful man because of the journey he'd taken. He realized he wouldn't have been developed enough to be with this lovely soul, a gentle plantswoman and landscape designer, if she'd arrived at the beginning of his search.

As Wally learned, persistence isn't just about keep-ing on keeping on. Persistence is itself an almost mys-tical process through which we develop ourselves and become accomplished, capable, and, in some situations, such as finding love, vulnerable enough to receive what we have been so persistently moving toward.

Persistence as a Gift

I was a young graduate student when my father died. I'd never watched a death before, and I can't say that I was exactly prepared for this one. Just as I had never lived through a death, my father had never gone through the process of dying, and I wondered how he would handle it. My father's great gift was his ability to communicate very directly with people, to speak the unvarnished truth, to engage in authentic emotional exchange. On the night he learned he didn't have long to live, he said sadly, "One hopes, always, for good news." But once he had assimilated this clearly not very good news, he proceeded to ask his doctor, very directly, just how long he might expect to live and what, exactly, were the stages he was likely to go through as he was dying.

One morning, close to the end, when his doctor came in to check his vital signs, my father, struggling, raised himself up in the bed. "Since you told me a couple of days ago that in a few more days I'll be in a coma," he said to the doctor, "I'd like to take this opportunity to thank you for everything you've done for me during these final days of my life."

The doctor was taken aback. First he tried to deflect my father's words by saying that, actually, he'd just stopped by to order a few more tests. As he was explaining rather lengthily about the nature of the tests, my father interrupted him and said, with his persistent directness, "I don't want any more tests. You told me a few days ago that I'm less than a week from my death. There's nothing more to figure out. What I really want to do is just to thank you and say good-bye."

Teetering half in and half out of the doorway to

my father's room, the doctor lost his composure, and a scattering of tears rolled down his cheeks. Finally he walked back into the room, stood at my father's bedside, and shook his hand. My father thanked him for having chosen to be a doctor, for having had the courage to treat people with terminal illnesses, for being so straightforward in communicating to him — and to us, his family — about the path of his illness, and for being so kind and consistent in his attending presence. At this, the doctor lost it. "Thank you," he said, now openly weeping. "Thank you very much."

A few weeks after my father died, I ran into his doctor. He told me my father had had a great impact on him; he'd never seen a person face his own death with such equanimity and directness. He said he'd struggled for years with telling people the truth about their condition, and that it had been my father's directness at the outset which had allowed him, at least part of the time, to be straightforward in his own communication. He then said that he'd recently been contemplating giving up on being a physician because the burden of not being able to speak the truth in the difficult circumstances of a terminal illness had become almost unbearable. But now, because of his engagement with my father, he had been able to integrate it.

Even as he was dying, my father persisted, living the way he had always lived. This had a great impact on at least one person's life, and as a consequence, I'm sure, on many other lives. As my father's journey shows, when we persist, it's not just that we reach our own goals, but our lives can also become vessels of teaching and giving for others. This happens by example through the very practice of our persistence and through whatever it is that we have chosen to persist in. So, for example, if you persist in joy through your crisis, you will inspire others to take heart. If you persist in working two jobs to pay off your credit card debt, you will model the possibility of becoming debt free. And if you persist in being a loving person, despite not having a sweetheart of your own, your life can become a living emblem of love.

Face the Music

Oliver, a gifted professional musician, lived in a house he had inherited from his father and mother. Grateful for the gift and wanting to expand his capabilities, he borrowed against the house and bought several hundred thousand dollars' worth of recording equipment so he could record his music at home. Like lots of remodeling projects, Oliver's studio went over budget, but, undaunted, he decided to rent out a bedroom so he could complete it.

As the house was being finished, and to celebrate his upcoming birthday, Oliver's girlfriend invited him on a trip across the country so he could visit, among other things, the birthplace of Elvis Presley. As they were traveling through the South, having lunch with old friends, Oliver fell backward into their empty swimming pool and broke his leg.

While racing to the hospital, Oliver suddenly had to confront the fact that he had no medical insurance. Surgery and reconstruction of his leg would cost him a small fortune, and when he finally did get back home, he realized, not only would he need to be under a doctor's supervision and have to undergo extensive physical therapy, but because of his limited movement he probably wouldn't be able to perform for over a year.

Oliver flirted with giving up in despair, but instead he decided to face the music and sell his house to pay for his medical bills. Unfortunately, since he'd lived there forever, it was crammed to the gills with his and his parents' things. He hired some helpers and, literally crawling around on the floor, often in excruciating pain, supervised the removal of truckloads of stuff. Then, making dozens of phone calls, he helped his tenant find a new place to live. His friends suggested that, now that his house was so cleaned up and beautiful, he ought to just stay there. Yet Oliver persisted in what he believed his crisis was asking of him; he put his house on the market. It sold in three days.

Persisting once again, he asked a friend to drive him around until he found an apartment. Deciding it could assist him with the rehabilitation of his leg, he chose a second-floor apartment reachable only by a long flight of steps. There, tottering around on his cane, he supervised still other helpers as they arranged all his things. When everything was settled, he sat quietly in his kitchen each morning, practicing his violin.

When it comes to persistence, the medium is certainly the message. Through the practice of persistence we become, moment by moment, more capable of enduring what we are going through as well as being transformed by it. There is a peace, a radiance, that comes from this. Oliver not only accomplished a move that, really, had needed to happen for a long time, but, in persisting through the crisis, learned to create the kind of soulful music he had never before considered composing.

Oliver's leg is healed now, and he's performing once again. His new studio, he says, is his new kitchen window.

❧ Persistence and You ❧

Persistence has an almost old-fashioned quality in this age of instant everything. But it is a powerful and graceful journey that brings strong results. Often when we need it most, though, we don't realize that its quiet steadiness will win the day. Pausing to note how and where you may need to persist right now will, I hope, strengthen the momentum of your progress.

- The area of your life in which you are most discouraged and to which you really need to bring the practice of persistence is _____. This could be dealing with health issues, looking for a job, or recovering from loss or death.

- For you, persistence in this area would consist of _____. Some examples would be: taking vitamins every day, sending out résumés every single morning, meditating regularly, or replacing every negative thought with a positive statement until your attitude improves.

- How long would you have to persist? For example, setting ninety days of not drinking as an initial goal. Or not using any credit cards until the entire balance on at least one of them has been paid off. What would be the first and smallest part of that goal that you would like to accomplish?

- What is the outcome you seek as a consequence of your persistence? For example, a real-live someone to have a relationship with, a new job, sobriety, or the loss of fifty pounds and the ability to maintain your new svelte body.

- What simple practice would help you stay on your path of persistence? For example, you could use a talisman to remind yourself of your commitment; make a simple "star chart," as if for a child, and give yourself a star for every day you succeed in your efforts; develop a new habit to replace the old one; chant, pray, recite an affirmation.

If you want to get through this crisis,
you will have to

Integrate Your Loss

CHAPTER 7

Integrate Your Loss

"Enlightenment doesn't occur from sitting around visualizing images of light, but from integrating the darker aspects of the self into the conscious personality."

— Carl Jung

In order to get through the crisis you're in, you will have to accept what has happened and then integrate it into the fabric of your life. Your integration of the content and the meaning of the crisis will be the sign, the hallmark, that you are moving through this challenge.

Integration is wholeness, the weaving together of opposites, the inclusion of what's been separated, denied, or excluded. Racial integration in American society occurred when buses, drinking fountains, and schools could no longer be legally separated by color; it is exemplified when a man of mixed race, of black and white parents, is elected president of the United States. On a personal level, emotional integration occurs when a person can both laugh and cry, be terrified and utterly at peace. Spiritual integration occurs when you can feel yourself as part of the unity of all humanity and the entire cosmos, and yet you can still get up in the morning and go to your factory job sorting widgets.

Crisis of any kind calls us to integration. In times of ease — a goose on every table, a car in every garage — we feel strong, practically invincible, able to plan and choose, control and decide, keep out what we want to keep out, let in only who or what we want to let in. In high times we are the architects of our castles, the captains of our yachts. We operate from the illusion that we actually are in control.

But when crisis comes, the kaleidoscope turns, and like Siddhartha stepping out of his father's beautiful palace one morning to discover death and pain, age and grief, we are suddenly awakened. We see that life is not just a blissful paradise, but a journey of difficulty and impermanence. And we have a choice then — to deny the difficulties that occur and wish they would all go away, or to integrate them into the larger quilt of our experience.

Integration always requires some kind of yielding

— getting over something you didn't want to get over, letting in something you wanted to keep out, seeing events from another perspective. True integration is a journey of ever-deepening acceptance, and it always has transformation as its consequence.

When we integrate loss, we include it in our perception of wholeness without erasing it. We don't dwell on it, but we know it is still there. We draw it into the circle of emotional healing where it can be transformed. Instead of being dogged by it, spending our energy trying to paper over or deny it, we find peace through a deeper — an integrated — acceptance of it. In order to do this, though, we must face it, own it, and find a place for it in our midst.

Facing it means telling yourself the truth about what has happened. Yes, I did suffer a permanent injury in the accident. Yes, I really did lose half my fortune. Yes, the man I was in love with has gone off and married somebody else. Owning it means "getting it" that there's no going back. Whatever happened was not a preview, a joke, or a rehearsal. It is now part of you and your story, and it's not going to change. Finding a place for it means realizing that through your loss you have been given an opportunity for transformation, seeing what that transformation has been, and then receiving its meaning.

When you have completed these three steps, you have integrated something as part of our being, and in one way or another, you have been transformed. Sometimes this transformation is a change in yourself: "I was texting while driving; that's why I had the accident. I'll never do that again." Sometimes it's a change in attitude: "I've always called truck drivers stupid, but it was a rancher with a truck who rescued me in the flash flood." And sometimes it's a change in action: "My son is dead, but as a consequence of what I learned about teenagers and depression, I started the teen suicide clinic."

Often the transformation is spiritual, an entirely new view of life and the world: "I used to feel so alone, but when I stood at the airport with all the others whose husbands and wives and children had also died in the plane crash, I grieved for us all. For the first time in my life I knew in a palpable way that we're all part of one another."

Our wholeness is the sum of all its parts, and even the parts we want to exclude are essential to that whole. When we integrate both our positive and negative experiences, we become more richly textured, stronger, more varied and complex human beings. When we integrate things that stretch our hearts to the limit and build our compassion, we grow as souls.

Achieving integration is a process. It isn't accomplished in a minute. It's a step-by-step journey, with many sequences of two steps forward, one step back. You visit and revisit the painful thing until finally you know it as part of your life and it has lost its hold over you. As you do the work of integration, you will gradually notice that you have been transformed by what has now been included. You have become greater than, or significantly different from, who and what you were before. Your picture of reality has been revised. Deep inside you feel a greater measure of peace.

When the disowned is owned, when the dark is nestled in the light, when the new and the old are holding hands, you will have moved to the place beyond your problem.

The Kaleidoscope

My parents' kaleidoscope was my early teacher of integration. It wasn't just a cheesy cardboard cylindrical tube with lots of little pieces of torn-up tissue paper inside like most kaleidoscopes nowadays. It was a big kaleidoscope with an impressive black leather–covered barrel, and its tube was a whopping five inches or so in circumference. It looked like a telescope, and it had its own very handsome wooden stand. You turned it with six notched brass spokes, reminiscent of a ship captain's wheel, that were stationed at one-inch intervals along the wide brass loop that surrounded the barrel.

I really loved this kaleidoscope, which, on quiet rainy Sundays, my parents would often bring out of the closet for us to enjoy. They'd stand it up on the living room floor, like a visiting guest almost, and one after another my brother, my sisters, and I would get to look through it, turn the wheel, and watch the infinite number of designs form and reform as all the pieces fell into place.

This fabulous kaleidoscope had many remarkable contents: a tube of glass with liquid that had a little bubble in it, like a carpenter's level, a small square piece of screen, pieces of lace and colored cloth, many colored bits of paper, sequins, one small nail, and what seemed to be a blue doll's eye.

I always wondered what the makers of the kaleidoscope could have been thinking when they decided to toss in that eye. It seemed so different, so anthropomorphic, so unlike all the rest of the bits of stuff that were circulating around inside. Because it always seemed so odd, so inconsistent with everything else, I was always trying to get rid of it, trap it under the wall of the mirrored channel or magically coax it to fall through the bottom, so it would stop distorting what I thought was the perfection of all of the other pieces in the design.

What never ceased to amaze me, though, was that no matter how I held the kaleidoscope, no matter how I might try to prejudice the projection of all the pieces inside it — tilt it sideways, lift one of the legs of the stand up really high, shake all the pieces down to one corner — all of the pieces, including, of course, the doll's eye, would always show up in the circle.

Then one day I noticed how interesting the doll's

eye looked, poised as it was for a nanosecond on top of the little square of screen. It looked almost beautiful, and in that moment I accepted it. I noticed, in the next turn of the wheel, that it looked interesting, too, against one of the pieces of lace, and I accepted it more. Finally, I realized that of course it belonged, that its jarring and sometimes beautifully mysterious humanness added a certain piquancy to the mix, that the kaleidoscope itself and my fascination with it would never have been what it was without the inescapably weird and beautiful doll's eye.

Just as my parents' kaleidoscope taught me that, in spite of my prejudice and distaste, everything inside it, including the doll's eye, belonged, your crisis is here to teach you about integrating whatever is hard for you to accept. It is here to remind you that life is a journey of emotional and spiritual evolution in which you are invited, step by step, increment by increment, to recognize the wholeness that is each of us and all there is. On a personal emotional level this journey of integration means coming to acknowledge more and more aspects of ourselves — the good, the bad, and the ugly; the simple, the outrageous, and the amazing. On a spiritual level it's a journey in which we become capable of integrating the opposites all around us — kindness and violence, sickness and health, light and dark, life and death — and seeing that they are all part of the vast, inclusive tapestry that is the whole of existence.

The more we are able to embrace, to *integrate*, these opposites, especially the ones that rattle our emotions and stretch our spirits, the more we see that everything and everyone belongs. We see that *because* of accepting our limitations, we can also celebrate our magnificence; *because* of violence, we are moved to tears by the unselfish gestures of heroes; *because* of the dark, we can see the light; and *because* of death, we can treasure the precious moments of life.

Accepting Darkness to Find the Light

For years Sally Anne had been a very successful real estate broker. Over a decade, she had single-handedly spearheaded the redevelopment of a historical neighborhood in her town, which over the years had fallen into ruins. Riding the wave of her remarkable success, she bought and renovated a huge downtown building, set herself up in its penthouse office, then bought herself an upscale condo.

Since she'd worked so hard for so long, she decided to start indulging herself. She took three extended holidays in a row, leaving her business in the hands of her associates. In the midst of this extended sojourn, one of her colleagues emailed her that there were signs of difficulty in the market. However, rather than taking this as a sign that she ought to get home, Sally decided to further extend her vacation; she went off to a remote village in Bali and completely stopped checking her email. Meanwhile, the real estate market plummeted. Sally Anne, soaking up her twenty-five-dollar massages and enjoying her much-needed rest, couldn't be bothered.

Sally Anne was unwilling to integrate the truth of what was happening, and so she returned to a decimated business. She never did financially recover from that vacation. Months later, some old health issues kicked in and she found herself hospitalized (with lapsed insurance), and she had to take out a huge personal loan to pay her hospital bills. Eventually she also had to sell the office building at a loss, vacate her condo (which was foreclosed upon), file for bankruptcy, and camp out on a friend's couch for over a year. Still struggling with health issues, she finally moved to a low-rent town where she knew absolutely no one. Friends who still hear from her say that all she ever writes about is "coming home" and waiting for "things to get back to the way they were."

Sally Anne has never integrated her experience.

Diandra was rendered a paraplegic in a devastating bicycle accident. This was followed by a heartbreaking and exhausting recovery, during which her parents never accepted her injury. They kept dragging her to magical people they were sure could "fix her so she could walk again."

At a certain point in our work together, Diandra

realized she was angry at all the people who refused to accept the magnitude and the permanence of her injury. This was the beginning of her healing. It allowed her to grieve. Her grief allowed her to accept her loss, which in turn allowed her to inquire about its possible meaning. Exploring what its message might be, she told me that she was a girl who had always had everything: beauty, money, boyfriends, health, and extraordinary athletic ability. Ironically, she said, she'd always believed her legs were so strong that they could carry her through anything. It was through losing the use of her legs that she finally realized that she was not in control.

As she moved through her crisis, she came to realize that the accident was a call to her soul's work, which was, as she put it, to be a living example of the truth that "we are more than the body." Grieving, accepting, seeing the meaning, Diandra integrated her loss. The miracle of her healing is that she lives in a state of radiant acceptance.

Diandra is a living example of tragedy transformed.

Sharon's husband was murdered while she watched from inside her car. One night when they were driving home from a summer vacation, they stopped at a small truck stop store to pick up some coffee and food, and a man who was holding up the store gunned down both Sharon's husband and the owner. Sharon's not sure she has or ever will actually "recover." The entire texture of her world has changed. "It's like trying to get over the impact of a neutron bomb," she says. Has she integrated the loss? As she says, "I'm simply putting one foot after another. Breathing." But now she knows how precious the gift of her thirty-two-year-long marriage was — something she'd always taken for granted — and how precious life itself is. "It's paradoxical," she says. "I've lost everything. Sometimes I don't even want to be alive. And yet, in a way I could never conceive of before, now every moment is precious."

Sharon has learned the exquisite value of life.

Rick had always worried about money. Driven by fear, he worked nonstop for twenty-five years, squirreling away funds for his retirement. When the stock market corrected in 2008 and he lost half his money, he realized that he had never enjoyed his life. For him, integrating the loss meant accepting the fact that he wasn't going to have a cushy retirement. Instead of rushing out to redouble his efforts, he moved to a small apartment and decided to make wind chimes, which is something he'd always wanted to do. Today, he sells his wind chimes on weekends at the beach.

For Rick, integrating the loss meant starting to live with joy.

Like the doll's eye in the kaleidoscope, the thing that is troubling you now, the thing that you wish had never happened, the thing you'd like to deny and forget, is now part of your life. It's not going anywhere. You have the choice of integrating your experience and learning from it or missing the chance. Perhaps, like Diandra, you have an opportunity to be transformed because of it. How will you choose?

The Full Scope of Integration

The work of integration is multifaceted. It includes accepting things from outside yourself — people, circumstances, ways of being — that are unfamiliar, scary, offensive, or just simply different. It also includes accepting the parts of yourself you'd like to disown. Right now, for example, you may find it difficult to accept the part of yourself that contributed to your crisis. Why didn't you save more money for a rainy day, take better care of your health, or leave the joker before he left you?

You will find clues about the things you need to integrate when you notice what you'd like to set aside, put on a shelf, or try to disown. The further you try to push these things away, however, the more you'll find them sticking to you, because, in fact, they're part of you. It is only through acceptance — through integration — that they can take the proper big or little place inside you that can make you whole.

Surprisingly, however, just as it's difficult to integrate aspects of ourselves or of life that we don't like, it's also very difficult for us to integrate the parts of ourselves that are deeply precious and of great value. There are lots of reasons why what's exceptional in us gets disowned. All of them, as you might imagine, have to do with our Life Themes — how our parents, siblings, teachers, and others disowned, undervalued, or just plain made fun of what was rare, beautiful, and ingenious about us. As a consequence of your theme, you may not feel worthy of the promotion you just got, or of the compliments you always receive, or of the handsome guy who just chose you, instead of the former prom queen, to be his date to the Black-and-White Ball. Integration isn't just about accepting the difficult, scummy, or threadbare parts of ourselves; it's also about accepting our grandeur, our magnificence, our brilliance, and our beauty. Surprisingly, this can often be just as difficult. Disowning your riches can also contribute to the hard times, crises, and spirit-rocking challenges in your life.

The Singer and the Song

Micah was an enthusiastic and musically talented young boy who, for the sheer joy of it, loved to sing to his mother. One day when he was doing just that, his older sister came around and asked him why he was being such an idiot and "screeching" at their mother like that.

Devastated, young Micah went to his room and lost himself in reading science fiction. But even so, as the years passed he kept being recognized as the "guy with the great voice" when he read aloud in his English classes. When he got to high school an English teacher recommended him for a theater arts class. There, after trying out for a minor part, he handily won the lead role in the school's production of *Brigadoon*, a musical with both speaking and singing parts. Overwhelmed by his selection, Micah went into disowning mode. He told his teacher that he had after-school work and tried to slouch into the understudy role, but his teacher had been bowled over by Micah's singing and insisted that he accept the lead. It would be a wonderful opportunity, the teacher told him, to develop this "hidden talent."

Connecting with his childhood trauma around his voice, Micah tried every which way to blow this opportunity — missing rehearsals, picking a fight with his co-lead, getting drunk with some friends one night. When the teacher finally confronted him about his "downright sabotage," Micah broke down and wept, telling the story about his sister and how for more than a dozen years he had tried to silence himself.

With his teacher's encouragement, Micah poured his heart out in the role. He got rave reviews — except from his sister, who decided to go on a camping trip the entire week of his performance. Micah felt celebrated and confirmed in the direction of his music, and he has since become a professional singer. However, he says that to this day it's always a bit of a challenge to perform without hearing his sister's critical voice. He's noticed, too, that over the years he's blown off several opportunities. After carelessly delaying the signing of a major contract that almost cost him a huge recording deal, he realized that he has to be constantly vigilant about his unconscious tendency to sabotage his talent.

Seeing the Bigger Picture

When less serious or even minor problems cause us to overreact or knock us far out of balance, it's another sign that integration is called for. Heather, for example, came to talk with me because she was devastated over the recent death of her cat. The kitten was less than six months old, and she'd painstakingly trained it to stay out of the street. One night, though, she heard her dog barking loudly at three in the morning, and she came outside to find that her cat had been flattened by a car.

She buried the cat in the backyard and "cried plenty," she said, but weeks later she was still devastated. She told me this wasn't the first of her cats that had died. When she was thirteen, one cat had suddenly died for no reason; another, when she'd gone away to college, had been eaten by coyotes. A third and fourth had disappeared when she'd moved to a new town.

She was angry. She told me she was never getting a cat again. They died. They disappeared. It wasn't fair. She hated being so vulnerable. On the other hand, she was miserable without a cat to enjoy. She didn't know what to do.

I suggested that maybe this series of losses was a preparation for some of the larger losses that are inevitable in life. By learning how to integrate this loss, she'd experience gratitude for the moments of joy her cats provided, and she'd also accept the normal circle of life and death.

Heather went away from that session a little disgruntled, but when she came back two weeks later, she looked happy. She'd had a good cry, she told me, and had gotten a new cat. She'd realized how ridiculous it had been to assume — to expect — that none of her cats would die. She had a greater reverence for life, she said, realizing how truly fragile it is, which was something she'd never wanted to face. In that session she also mentioned offhandedly that her father was getting old, that they had been estranged for years, and that maybe she'd better go see him.

I didn't see Heather again for almost a month.

When I did, she told me that, in spite of her lifelong irritation with him, she'd gone to see her father. They had the only "almost meaningful" conversation they had ever had. The following morning he had a stroke, and two days later he died.

Heather told me that, had she not integrated the notion of impermanence, she would "never have been able to handle" her father's sudden death. Having the courage to integrate these many small losses had helped her accept not only her father's death but also their imperfect relationship.

Integrating Your Relationships

Megan came to see me because, after two "heartbreaking" relationships had ended, she found herself falling in love with another man. She was scared, she told me. She didn't want to get hurt again. She said she'd "wasted a lot of good years" on the two relationships that had ended and she didn't want to "waste any more time."

I pointed out to Megan that she had basically disowned both of her previous relationships. She was treating them like bad things that she had to take a stand against, things that should never have happened. She said this was true; she did wish they had never happened and she definitely didn't want something like that to ever happen again.

When we talked about the details of these relationships, though, it was clear that the first had involved a very healing connection. In it, she'd experienced the steady love and daily stability that she had never experienced as the child of two alcoholics. When it ended, she had gone on to have a passionate romance that engaged her sensuality in a delicious and joyful way, although it was clear from the beginning that this man would never be a life partner.

When I suggested to Megan that she integrate these relationships as part of the whole life story of her relationships, she relaxed. Instead of judging herself — and the men — for being wrong, she realized that she and they had been on a journey together. Now, with the new man she was falling in love with, that journey would continue.

Instead of continuing to disown her past relationships, Megan was finally able to integrate them. As a consequence, she was able to welcome this new relationship into her life. A year later when I ran into her on the street, she told me that she was happily married.

Crisis cajoles us to move toward integration, to expand, to accept more. This process of acceptance is not incidental to a challenging time; it is one of its intended purposes. That is because, while our human nature prefers distinction, separation, and confusion, our spiritual nature seeks wholeness, inclusion, and union. Since we are ultimately spiritual in nature, life keeps pointing us in the direction of this growth. Like the kaleidoscope, it keeps offering us the pieces that we must put together.

Integration can arrive in an instant, when, through the free fall of surrender, you finally accept each one of the parts of your existence, even the ugly ones, even the irritating ones, even the ones you want to negate, destroy, and disown. Or it can come more slowly, as day by day, episode by episode, you gradually come to accept what has happened. When you do, you become whole. You become whole not because you have finally gotten rid of the painful or offensive item, not because you have escaped, but because you have embraced it. This is the process of integration in ourselves, in others, in the world. When we have achieved full integration, we know that there is only wholeness, which is enlightenment itself.

Moving toward integration, to the space in yourself where you can see the wholeness of life, gives you a sense of hope. It also brings great peace because you know that your life, even in this crisis, and your soul, for all eternity, are nestled in the blanket of wholeness where everything, even this very difficult time, has its perfect place.

⤖ Integration and You ⤕

As we have seen, integration is a process of inclusion. Becoming aware of, accepting, and finding a place for whatever has been hard to integrate in the past is a natural and important part of healing from your crisis. By doing so, you can find a new level of peace. Here are some questions to help you with that undertaking.

- What is the crisis, the difficult experience, the loss or change of status that you are trying to integrate right now? For example: "I've just lost my house." "I've just been fired." "My fiancé ran off with my best friend." "I've been diagnosed with a chronic illness."

- Ask yourself if you have accepted it yet — that it happened, that it's not going to go away, that you will have to deal with it.

- If you think about this experience as holding a deeper meaning for you to integrate, what would it be? That is, what is your difficult experience asking you to understand, grow toward, be aware of, or become? For example: "This is teaching me about my vulnerability — I always try to be strong, when in fact I have some very weak and scared parts, too. I'm more vulnerable than I imagined."

- What is the transformation you are already experiencing as a consequence of what you are going through? What is the further transformation, the outcome or change that you seek?

For example: "As a consequence of accepting my diabetes diagnosis, I've become extremely conscious of my health. I have really started taking care of myself in ways I never did before. Now, instead of seeing medication as a quick-flash remedy, I've taken on the project of my well-being as a lifelong enterprise."

If you want to get through this crisis,
you will have to

Live Simply

CHAPTER 8

Live Simply

"Do what you can. Where you are. With what you have."

— Theodore Roosevelt

Living simply is paring away — stuff, obligations, expectations, people. It's removing all the glut and rubble from your life, making space in your house, your heart, your brain, and your life for exactly and only what you need. It's getting down to the core of things and returning to a way of living that most of us can only vaguely remember: pleasures that don't cost piles of money, rewards you don't have to buy in stores, amusements that don't require a screen or scrabbling with hundreds of other people to get to.

When I say live simply, I'm not talking about picking up a copy of one of those make-your-life-simple magazines at the checkout counter of the health food store for $4.95 and doing all the really pretty expensive things they tell you to do, like paint every piece of your living room furniture the same uplifting color of pea green. I'm talking about the practice of simplicity in all its forms as a kind of human grace and peace, about being present in every moment with the softest, smallest thing you can be present with — washing dishes, taking out the trash, choosing what you wear and eat and listen to, what you choose to throw away, what you save and use again. Simplicity can be as simple as sweeping the leaves from the path and using them to mulch the ferns, cutting up your old T-shirts and using them for rags, refolding and reusing a brown paper bag.

When we live with simplicity we gain a sense of hope because at some level we really do know that we're all in this together. There is a sickening discomfort in our souls that comes from continually taking and using more than our fair share. The more of us who live simply, the more we can imagine that somehow we, as a species, might actually dig ourselves out of the landfill and climate change nightmares we have created by being such overindulgent pigs.

We feel good — hopeful, alive, optimistic — when we live simply because we can relax, knowing that we're part of the solution and not part of the problem. We are not putting ourselves or the rest of the world in jeopardy by taking more than what is rightly ours. When we live simply we are able to rest in the peace that simple living brings: a quieting of the endless mental chatter and the agitation to have more, a simplicity of movement and action in the passage of each day. Time to sit still, to talk with your children, to stare into your lover's eyes, to read a book, to water a tree, to pray.

Simplicity and Hard Times

It's good to live simply when things are going well, but when life is difficult, it is essential. That's because every object, habit, movement, conversation, undertaking, responsibility, and reaction takes energy. The more people, circumstances, widgets, emails, objects, people, and tasks you're dealing with, the less energy you have. If your daily to-do list is already burning up all the calories you can cobble together from dawn till dusk on a "normal" day, where are you going to get the extra energy to deal with the flood in the basement, the banker banging at the door, all those extra trips to the lab and the X-ray department when the unbearable, or the unexpected, shows up in your life?

We are energetic beings, and in a single life we get only so much energy. Do you want to use yours sorting out your storage — as one person I know does practically every Saturday, rooting through her mother's old tablecloths — or do you want to go fishing, feel the beauty of your humanity, breathe in the majesty of the elm trees, see the bleeding colors of the sunset? We came to life not to be saddled with junk, but to feel ourselves and the mystery of life. You will need to live simply through this crisis or else you won't have enough energy to get through it. Once you have lived through it, you will understand more about what's really important in life. In fact, maybe that's why it showed up in the first place.

Our life's purpose is not simply to amass more and more stuff, but in spite of the attraction of all our stuff, the seduction of all our material attachments, to connect with the depth of who we are. If you don't live with simplicity through these hard times, chances are you won't make it through. Instead of being a teaching, an opportunity, or a transformation, the terrible thing you're going through now will chew you up and spit you out: sick, addicted, friendless, bitter, maybe even suicidal or dead. Is it worth it, hanging on to every little thing you're attached to, when, simply by having the courage to cut through some of the caked-on layers of stuff, you can regain your energy? Your disaster is asking you to learn to live simply so that, instead of being a dead-end trip, it can become the doorway to a powerful new chapter of your life.

The Most Challenging Place to Live Simply

The hardest place to live simply is in the realm of our possessions. Most of us are addicted to having and spending, and as a consequence, we are often possessed by our possessions. As a society, we are just beginning to learn how to have less, just starting to consider that not only do we need to recycle our old stuff but we actually need to diminish the amount of stuff we each possess.

Indeed, I've often wondered how it is that we Americans can so cavalierly let go of our relationships — 50 percent of first marriages end in divorce, and an even higher percentage of second and third marriages do — and yet we find it so hard to get rid of our stuff. How is it that we let go of people but hang on to things? In theory, we have our most significant connections with people, but we have such a tenacious, one-directional, desperate connection to our stuff that it almost seems as if, in a divorce, we work harder to save our possessions than our relationships. We wrangle over the flat-screen TV, the Mark Rothko painting, the silver and china. In our profound emotional poverty, we come to believe that it is really stuff — rather than a vital, vulnerable engagement with another human being — that brings us joy, meaning, and contentment.

Who ever died happy because they had ten million things in their storage locker? Because they got the spoils of their divorce? Because they had twenty of everything to choose from?

It's beautiful and even important to let go. When you get rid of your stuff, you're doing a couple of really great things. You are lightening your material burden, and you're making room for something other than your possessions to take up your time, fill up your heart, and get your attention. The truth is, if you can let go of people, of the man or woman you thought you'd be married to forever, then you can also get rid of the George Foreman grill, the clothes you haven't worn for six years, and the camping tent you never use. Especially right now, when somebody else could really use them.

It's Complicated to Simplify Your Life

It isn't easy to live simply. Everything in our world conspires against it. Our enormously productive economy demands that we make consumption our way of life, that we convert the buying and use of goods into rituals, that we seek our spiritual satisfaction, our ego satisfaction, in consumption. Consider these stunning facts:

- Each person in the United States makes more than four pounds of garbage per day.

- Each person in the United States is subjected to three thousand advertisements in a day.

- Americans, collectively, have accumulated more than $9 billion in credit card debt.

In part, we've been tricked. The dog-eared saying that less is more promises that, Bingo! when we have less, we will automatically have more — more time, more space, more depth, more serenity. But, in fact, this takes a lot of work. You have to take real-life steps to have less, and this is a thoughtful and time-consuming process. You have to think, decide, choose, and act in every minute about what you are going to hold on to and what you want to let go of. Then you have to consciously take steps to acquire more peace and focus. The fruits of simplicity don't just show up on your doorstep because you've noticed you need a new hairbrush. If you want more time, you have to systematically avoid reading every brain-infesting news flash that wiggles its way into your world; you have to stop giving hours of attention to the headlines that pop up on your internet homepage. If you want more space, you have to dismantle all the old paint cans that are holding up the walls of your garage like the pillars of the Parthenon, find the location of the toxic waste drop-off, then load the cans in your car and actually haul them over there. If you want more breathing room in your bedroom, you have to go through the clothes in your closets and drawers — then consider, decide, toss, recycle, and reorganize.

We didn't bring the planet to its knees, spitting out hurricanes, coughing up floods, wheezing with forest fires, in just a decade. It will take decades of concentration — of love, really — to return the earth to her grace. If we as human beings are going to survive, we need to do more than romantically entertain the idea of having less. We have to understand that our self-indulgence has practically devoured us, and that it's high time to get over it. We have to surrender to not just the beauty but the necessity of simplicity; it has to become our daily practice. Moment by moment, we have to choose to have less, and once again we have to surrender to the organic order of things, the relationship between seedtime and harvest, between having less and finding peace, between silence and deep inner well-being. If we don't, not only will we find ourselves taxed, exhausted, and dispirited, but ultimately, like the cat who endlessly roughs up the mouse until it lies crumpled and dead in the corner, we shall have ruined beyond repair this beautiful creature we live on.

Beneath Your Cluttered Life
Lies a Simple One

Ted, a successful magazine writer and literary aficionado, is now an expert on the effort it takes to get to less. More than twenty years ago, he moved into the apartment of his dreams in one of the lovely old neighborhoods of Los Angeles. Since he was a lover of books, one of the first things he did was to have an accomplished carpenter build floor-to-ceiling bookcases on the longest unobstructed wall of his new living room. There, over the years, he ensconced his vast collection of books, the ones he already owned and the thousands more he acquired while he was living there.

Eventually, along with his books, Ted amassed a worthy collection of the many other tools of his trade: cameras, video and audio tapes of people he had interviewed, fancy storage systems for his documents, and a pretty respectable wardrobe. From time to time, over the years, he'd mention that his living room was "getting a little messy." One night he mentioned that he could no longer even remember the color of his living room carpet, since there seemed to be twenty-four piles of papers, magazines, and newspapers randomly arranged across it.

Then last summer Ted had a health scare. Walking home from a concert one night, he found himself out of breath, then keeling over on the sidewalk. He picked himself up and was escorted home by some kindly strangers. On a follow-up visit to the doctor, he discovered that his blood pressure was through the roof, as was his cholesterol; he was borderline diabetic and the perfect candidate for a heart attack.

His best friend, Marla, suggested that Ted come and live in her spare bedroom. She herself was in a financially lean time, and the two of them agreed it might be a good arrangement. As he started preparing for the move, Ted realized that he was awash in a sea of possessions. He spent days packing up all his books, most of which he'd never read; he'd simply collected them because at the time he'd had the money. The more he sorted and packed, the more overwhelmed he felt. One day he said that he felt as if his living room was cluttered with the remains of a "Satanic Christmas," a diabolical flood of gifts he'd never needed and never used. In despair, he spoke of how much money he'd wasted and of all the energy it was taking him now to get rid of all this "useless stuff." He put boxes of books on the curb for people in his neighborhood, took others to the used book store, sold others over the internet — a process which in itself was wildly exhausting.

A month after he started this grueling process, Ted had reduced his possessions to less than a tenth of what they had been. He kept only the few things that he needed to carry on with his work as a writer. As he sat in his relatively empty, now Zen-like living room — about to move into a single large room in Marla's apartment — he felt, he told me, an amazing sense of peace. "This place is really beautiful — now that I can see the floor and the walls," he said. "It's ironic. I spent years collecting all this stuff, when, actually, this is the feeling I was looking for all along."

What Would I Need from Here?

A couple of weeks ago, I went to the mall with a friend. I don't go to malls often, but on this particular afternoon I went because I needed a new battery charger for my cell phone. At the store I learned that my cell phone model had, basically, gone out with the mastodons; I'd have to contact the manufacturer, who "probably wouldn't have a battery charger for you either," the clerk said. After that hot bit of news, I turned to my companion and asked him, since we were at the mall, if he'd like to do a little shopping. Without skipping a beat, he turned to me and said emphatically, "Why? What would I need from here?"

How shocking! I thought. How delightful! How amazing! Indeed, what did he or I *need* from there? The minute he made his astonishing remark, I could feel the long-standing insidious impact of those three thousand advertisements a day. Like opium dens with their intoxicating vapors swirling around and luring us in, the malls in our midst have addicted us into believing that we've just got to have whatever we see. How utterly insane! When and how did we ever stop thinking — or, more importantly, *feeling* — for ourselves? When are we going to understand that we really do have to start having less, that contraction, conservation, and conscience must guide us as we take the next steps on our communal human journey?

There isn't enough of anything — coal, oil, water, trees, iron ore — to last humanity for eternity unless we curb the dogs of our self-indulgence and start planting back and putting back, unless we have the courage, the grace, the will to live with less.

It's urgent and it's time.

How about turning every mall into an organic garden? Asparagus for concrete, anyone? Tomatoes for asphalt? How delicious — how truly sacred — would that be?!

Sometimes a Little Is Enough

Years ago I had some friends who had an old tumble-down weekend house in the mountains of Appalachia. I spent a number of weekends there one summer, helping them scrape the old wallpaper from the inside plaster walls in preparation for replacing it with new. Given the gorgeous landscape, the charming old house, the interestingly craggy and beautiful faces of the people we passed on the way to my friends' house, I once invited another friend, a photographer, to join us for a weekend, so he could photograph some of the amazing faces in the neighborhood.

A city slicker and highly successful commercial

photographer, my friend did join us there one weekend. He was touched by the beauty of the land and deeply affected by the conditions in which the local people lived. Photographing a beautiful tangle-haired little girl one afternoon, as she sat in a raggedy blue flowered dress on the broken-down steps of the shack her family called home, he finally couldn't restrain himself. "Don't you just hate it, being so poor?" he finally asked her. "Don't you just wish you could go out and buy some new things?"

"I'm not poor," the little girl said defensively, looking at the photographer as if he were a lunatic. Then, reaching into the pocket of her dress she held up a white rabbit's foot. "I got this lucky rabbit's foot right here that my Daddy got me one day at the fair."

I'm sure that as time went on the little girl discovered that she did, in fact, need a few more things than a magic rabbit's foot, and I hope with all my heart that she got them. What I found remarkable about her, though, was that she had her priorities in order. She understood even then what she needed most was her father's love. And all these years later, my photographer friend still refers to her as his first spiritual teacher.

Unlike the little girl in the shabby blue dress, a lot of us could do with a little reprioritizing. Day by day, what are you choosing to value above all else?

Making Something out of Nothing

When I was in eighth grade, I spent a bunch of autumn weeks walking door to door with my sister and some of our friends to collect newspapers for the school paper drive. I can still remember the tangy slap of the fall air as we walked through the dark every night after school, plodding our way through the neighborhood; the flood of warm yellow light as the people inside, hearing our knocks or the sound of the doorbell, would turn on their porch lights and open their front doors to invite us, maybe a foot's worth, into their cozy heated living rooms. We would stand there and wait while the housewives and sometimes even their slightly disgruntled husbands would gather up all the loose papers from beside the father's sagging stuffed chair, or from the low-lying coffee table in front of the couch across from the mahogany TV console, and hand them over to us.

We pulled the papers home in my brother's red wagon, put them in big cardboard cartons or stacked them in pretty, neat piles, and then tied them in bales with strong white string. We stacked all the boxes and bales in the backseat of the family car, and every morning, my mother would drive us, along with our bales of papers, to school.

For more than a month, there was a great big old open-topped semi parked in the school yard, and every morning as all the cars pulled up, the senior boys on the ground would pass or throw the bales and boxes of papers up to the senior boys standing on top of the growing mountain of papers in the belly of the semi.

I felt so proud at the end of the month when I learned that our class had won the prize for the most pounds of paper collected, and that with all the money that all the grades together had earned, we were going to be able to buy a whole new set of uniforms and four new balls for our basketball team. A couple weeks later, the principal hired a very steady-handed painter who repainted all the worn-out lines of the basketball court – – black and very bright red — and revarnished the thrashed oak gymnasium floor. And two months later, for the very first time in the history of the world, our school's team won the all-state high school basketball championship.

I still get misty when I think about the paper drive. I'm touched, I suppose, because I think of how much was accomplished with so little. I think about how something basically useless created a new beginning. How being good stewards of what we have is a sacred act.

There's so much you can do with so little. If only you do it.

Whatever Happened to Heloise?

Whatever happened to Heloise, the witty journalist who used to tell us how to cut our SOS pads into three or four pieces so the big pad wouldn't rust all at once and be totally wasted all in one shot? Whatever happened to darning socks, wearing a sweater until it had a hole in it, mending the hole, and then wearing it again? Whatever happened to having a string box? Saving an envelope? Folding a brown paper bag on its creases and using it a second or third time?

Whatever happened to clothespin bags? To hanging your clothes outside on a line to dry? To the reweaving shops that could disappear that ugly cigarette hole in your woolen tweed skirt? To drinking ice water in summer instead of constantly running the air conditioner? To turning the lights off in the rooms you're not sitting in? To eating leftovers? Building compost heaps? Saving the pumpkin seeds to grow next year's jack-o'-lantern?

Whatever happened to the notion of conservation, to the idea that a little is enough? To the prayer that says thank you instead of please, that asks on behalf of others the same things that we ask for ourselves? These practices, these principles, are all as close as our fingertips, and yet none of them are trivial, incidental, or unimportant. Indeed, they are some of the smallest changes we can make that will have the largest impact. When you dedicate yourself to doing all the little things that allow you to live more simply, you're not just clearing space and lightening the load for yourself;

what you're doing represents nothing less than an act of love toward all of us.

What are the steps, the intricate little practices that can move you toward simplicity? You can buy reusable shopping bags or fold up your large paper bags and use them again. You can clean all the gook out of all the bottles and jars you recycle so they can actually be recycled. You can grow two beautiful food plants and share the fruits with your neighbors. You can change all your lightbulbs to fluorescent and put little signs on all your light switches so you remember to turn out the lights. You can use organic cleaning products. You can keep an empty shelf in one of your kitchen cupboards, so you can see and feel what an empty cupboard looks like — peace to the eyes, and gratitude for plenty. This will quietly remind you of all the people who actually don't have anything to put in their cupboards (to say nothing of all the people who don't even have a cupboard to put things in). And then, inspired by all this emptiness, you can donate the food you would ordinarily put on this shelf to your local food bank.

Every day you can act in useful, helpful ways to simplify your life. Taken together, these little actions could mean the difference between getting through your crisis or not. It could even mean the difference between life and death.

❧ Living Simply and You ❧

There is both a general urgency and immediate personal payoffs for living simply. When we simplify our lives, we become more available to other life experiences. What these new opportunities might be will only be revealed once you've taken the steps to simplify your life. Imagining the peace, the energy, and the surprises that await you as a consequence of choosing to live more simply, how would you answer the following questions?

- What are ten things you could get rid of immediately? Who could you give them to, so they remain helpful and useful, rather than throwing them away to join the 99 percent of manufactured goods that are in landfills? Can you commit to getting rid of ten things every week or once a month?

- What is an ongoing practice of conscious simplicity that you'd be willing to commit to, starting today? For a beginning list of ideas, see the "Whatever Happened to Heloise?" section above.

- What are the rewards — concrete, emotional, and spiritual — that you would like to receive from this committed movement toward simplicity? Spending less of your time dealing with possessions? Saving money? Living in a less cluttered and more beautiful environment? Cultivating a feeling of well-being, of sharing with others, of personal responsibility for the environment? Having more resources — ideas, energy, money — to focus on your current crisis or on other important problems? Increasing your spiritual connection to others and your community? Increasing the sense of peace in your own life?

If you want to get through this crisis,
you will have to

Go Where the Love Is

CHAPTER 9

Go Where the Love Is

"In times of crisis, love must prevail."

— Linda Laurie

There's a reason why so many of us are going through crises of one sort or another, why even as a nation and a global community we're facing such huge difficulties. Quite simply, we're in all this hell to bring us together, to remind us of the common thread of our humanity, to teach us to love. When our lives are no longer a walk in the park, we finally get it that we're all connected. We are not alone in the practice of our excesses, and we are not alone in our suffering.

Finally, we come face-to-face with our need. And with our need for each other.

My curmudgeonly Uncle Johannes used to say that human beings are a deplorable species. What he meant, I think, is that we can be an unconscious, self-focused, war-mongering species, that unlike dogs, for example, we often have to be jolted into acting with love. We have to be strafed into finding our capacity for compassion, battered into finding the wellsprings of our generosity. Left to our own devices, we can be narcissistic, greedy, and self-serving. But give us a good life-shaking crisis, and we wake up to the fact that we're all in this together. Misery teaches. Crisis inspires. Heartache breaks our hearts open to spilling.

In "interesting" times, when crisis comes upon us, we are awakened to the reality of suffering. What used to be invisible, hidden behind high walls and closed doors, is leaking out through lives all around us. Feeling our own pain, we start to notice the other troubled people in our midst. When you see that the person next to you in the grocery store, for example, is having a hard time deciding which items to buy and which to leave behind, or when you notice that there's a new man at your corner, begging with his cardboard sign, you suddenly "get it" that at the most basic day-to-day level a lot of us are struggling. The other person's struggle may not be the same as yours, but now you notice it. Your heart is touched, and you're a little more willing to share your money, your meals, your tears.

This is the way in which, day by day, circumstance by circumstance, we start to glimpse our interconnectedness, and this is how our consciousness starts to change. When we see our own journey of struggle and fear, anxiety and pain, reflected in the eyes and the anguish of another, we are moved from isolation to empathy. We actually start to live the truth that no one is an island. Suddenly we realize that everything we do or fail to do for our brothers and sisters affects the great body of us all. The debilitating illness you got from living in the mold-infested apartment your landlord neglected gets you to thinking about how the person who flushes his leftover antibiotics down the toilet in Urbana, Illinois, is affecting a stranger somewhere down the Mississippi — about how the corporation that muddies the air with its tons of toxins is poisoning the people who live in the town downwind, how the aerosol spray cans used in Tucson are enlarging the hole in the ozone layer, melting the ice floes in Antarctica, and obscenely increasing the rates of skin cancer in Australia. Seeing all this, finally noticing all this, you realize that at the end of the circle of all of our actions is a person who is one of us, a person who could be you.

When we're beset by crisis, we also begin to recognize our own vulnerability. We see that in one realm or another we, ourselves, could use some assistance. And so, from the chalice of our own need, we start reaching out for help. That's because once we've been taken apart by life, we are more humble, more open, more willing to both give and receive. We take bigger chances. We speak up. We reveal ourselves. We ask. We break down. We accept comfort. Words. A blanket. A meal. In time, we realize that something amazing has happened: that the more we reach out to others, the less lonely we feel ourselves. Somehow, even in the midst of our chaos, we are actually feeling loved. And the beautiful thing is that, the more love we need, suddenly the more love we have to give.

Learning to love, loving more, that's the bottom line of what a crisis is really all about. Through it, we are being asked to expand beyond the inordinate focus on ourselves — our obsession with what we need, want, and desire — to notice what we can share, how we can serve and be of help to one another. In short, we are being asked to enlarge the circle of our love. Of course, it's not always easy to do this. It may be unfamiliar. But when we do engage, when we see and hear and respond to one another, life starts to seem less scary. The more you get and give help, the more it seems that you will actually make it through your own unbelievably painful passage. You sense that there really is a new future. Even in the heartbreaking present you realize that you're not alone. Not only that, but instead of wearing out your biceps holding up a thousand-pound iron defense shield in front of your heart, you can let down your guard, let down your hair, give up your pride, have a good cry, and, in gratitude, receive the love that's coming toward you.

The Road to Love

I often walk on the beach near my home. The road that leads to this particular beach ends in a cliff-like drop-off that ordinarily you have to jump down in order to reach the sand below. One day last week as I was walking, I noticed a bunch of men lined up from the end of the road to the beach below, passing stones hand over hand up to one another. When I looked a little more closely, I could see that they were packing the stones into rows in the sand, covering them up with more sand, then smoothing the sand out on top to create a nice smooth sloping path from the end of the road to the beach down below.

Intrigued, I finally asked one of them what they were doing. "It's for Joe's grandma," the man named Pete told me, pointing uphill to Joe, one of the guys still packing sand and shuffling stones. "It's her ninety-third birthday. She took care of a lot of us when we were a bunch of hell-raising teenagers in Compton. She just got enrolled in hospice to take her finals, and yesterday she called Joe with a last request. She asked if he could get her down to the beach so she could see just one more sunset." She was still sitting "up there," Pete explained, in her wheelchair up in Joe's car, and they had built this road for her. In a couple more minutes, they were going to wheel her down to the water's edge for a sunset birthday party.

You may not, like Joe's grandma, be in the final weeks of your life, but if you're reading this book, your circumstances probably have an *in extremis* quality. What do you need? Who do you need to ask for exactly the piece of love you need right now? And do you have the guts, vulnerability, and humility to reach out and ask for it?

A Perfect Figure Eight

I have a friend, a French journalist, who always says that "everyone should take care of everyone." I was reminded of his words many times this past year, watching a woman named Lacey move through a lot of very hard days following her breast cancer diagnosis. At the time of the diagnosis, she lived alone in a neighborhood full of apartments and basically knew no one. Friends from where she used to live were always good about calling while she was going through what she euphemistically called her "treatments," but there were times, she told me, when she was brought to her knees by the pain and loneliness.

One afternoon when she was taking her dog for a walk, she noticed a woman moving into a nearby apartment. Lacey was touched when she saw this woman, seemingly also by herself, directing the movers as they unloaded boxes and furniture into the upstairs apartment. So, although she wasn't feeling that great herself, she went over to greet the woman and ask if she might be of some help. The woman said that she'd like it a lot if maybe she could just come by and have a cup of tea. She'd recently gotten divorced, she told Lacey, and this new apartment was really a come-down from the family home that she and her former husband had just put on the market. She was struggling to digest the facts of her diminished new life.

Lacey and Margaret had tea that first afternoon and during lots of afternoons after that. Margaret, it turned out, was a massage therapist, and between Lacey's chemotherapy sessions, she would stop over from time to time and work on Lacey's back and shoulders, easing the pain. Meanwhile, in an effort to boost her health while going through treatment, Lacey would haul herself out of bed every morning, walk down to the local produce store, and make several quarts of fresh vegetable juice. Each time she did, she'd bring some over to Margaret, as extra nourishment before she began her day.

Six months after she'd moved there, and after Lacey's treatments were finished, Margaret came home unexpectedly early one day and rapped on Lacey's door. She'd just gotten results from a routine mammogram; she, too, had been diagnosed with breast cancer. The two had a good cry, and some tea, and Lacey, whose hair had by then grown in red and strong, comforted Margie as she went through her own treatments. Lacey told her then, and she's told her every day since, "This is what people do for each other. I love you. And of course you can make it. Just look at me."

Margaret and Lacey held each other through their pain, with words and gestures and generosity and presence. They showed each other — and they show us — that what we do for each other reveals how precious we are.

Love Is All Around You

The only thing that can touch our pain, the only thing that can fix anything, really and forever, is love. Right this minute there are people you don't even know who are carrying you with their love. They are the men and women who work into the wee hours of a frozen morning bagging the sand so your house won't get carried downriver; the firemen with smoke in their eyes who put their lives on the line to save your house; the farmers who bring their organic lettuces and beets to your local farmers' market; the singers who, in the lonely hours, are singing you their song.

Their love can't erase all the terrible circumstances in your life. They can't yank your house back from the jaws of foreclosure, bring your wife back from her lover, your child back cured from the leukemia ward. But their love can enter the circle of your pain and quietly transform it. It can make you feel — for a minute, for an hour, for the duration of the hell you're in — a little less lonely on the path.

Dogs and cats can love you. Nature can love you. Music that sounds like you've heard it your whole life can love you. Art can love you. Beauty can love you. Whenever you deliver yourself to the experiences, sights, and sounds that make you feel loved, your experience will change. Your problems won't be instantly solved, but in the arms of love, they will start to feel different. *You* will feel different. Instead of being in the foreground, your difficulties will recede into the background and your experience of your catastrophe will be transformed. That's because Love is the highest vibration in this universe, and when you can feel it for even a nanosecond, everything else in your life will fall into its proper — and lesser — place.

Of course, we don't want love just in the abstract and in general. We want it to be personal and particular. That is, we want to feel and share love with real people in our lives. As you're going through this extremely difficult time, therefore, lean on the people who love you. Run, walk, or hopscotch, take a train, a plane, or a bus, to the people who can give you some love. They are your family, your friends, your neighbors and colleagues. Sometimes they're even strangers. Whoever they are, you'll know them by how they make you feel. With them, you feel happy and whole. They are the people who recognize your spirit, who touch your sensitivity, who nourish and enliven your body, who make you laugh, who "speak your language," who share your interests, who ask how you're doing, who call to see if you got the job, won the case, could get the car fixed for less than six thousand dollars.

They are the ones who say the words that will carry you through, who show up with the name of the doctor you need for a second opinion, the homeopathic remedy you've never heard of, the desk chair on Craigslist that's a perfect bargain, the apartment downstairs that's just become available. They will adopt your dog when you've lost your house to foreclosure, tell you they love you (with or without words), take you in when you can't pay your rent, help you make some extra money, and share the food from their garden.

But what if — alas and God forbid — you don't have a whole pack of people in your personal love corral to call on? What if you've been so sick that you haven't been out of your apartment to see the light of day for twelve months? What if you just moved from a thousand miles away? Then, instead of checking your corral, you will have to look for your hearth.

The Power of the Hearth

When I was hiking last fall with my suffering friend who inspired The Ten, I was reminded of the power of the hearth. We'd driven up to the mountains one day, then walked down a long, circuitous trail. At the end of it, on the crest of a mountain overlooking the vast valley below, were the ruins of what must have once been a great mansion. You could see, from the shape of the foundation, that its rooms once had views that ranged out over the whole expanse of the valley. But the most remarkable thing was that only the stones of its hearth were still standing — the chimney, a lonely stone sentinel, looking over the green valley below.

As we stood there, I was thinking of the similarity between the words *hearth* and *heart*, and of how, indeed, the hearth is the heart of the house, its pulse, its lap, its warmth. A hearth is the place where people gather, in silence or with words, to warm their bodies, to heal their hearts. Hearths are what we come home to, where we can rest, where we can sit together mesmerized, inspired by the flickering blue-and-orange flames. We are tribal animals and we find comfort — indeed, we find ourselves — in the warmth of one another. Human beings need hearths, especially in hard times. But just as a lot of houses no longer have hearths, a lot of lives don't have them either.

That's because the modern tribe, the nuclear family, has been decimated by changes in society and in our circumstances. We can have virtual conversations at any hour of the day or night on the internet. But our need for real human connection has not changed. We still have a profound need to gather, to feel the warmth of connection; in times of trouble especially, we need to gather at the hearth.

If you don't have an actual hearth, you can create a hearth for yourself. Any place you go to find comfort, to be reminded that you're not alone, can become your hearth. A hearth can be any place, public or private, where you can go to get a sense of belonging. It's your corner coffeehouse, your particular strip of beach, the bench where you always wait for the bus and pause to have a few words with the other people who ride it. It can be your church (or the church you still haven't joined), your AA meeting, your Weight Watchers group, or the hiking trail where you can soak up the sun and the scents of nature among fellow hikers. It can be a yoga class, the reading room in your library, or even the unemployment line.

I've even heard that in some cities people have "cuddle parties." These are gatherings where, in the presence of clearly defined sexual boundaries, folks fitful and frazzled by life get together to have a good cuddle or two. Recognizing the primal need for human touch, for connection and warmth, these people spend an evening together in someone's home, sometimes with music, often in silence, just holding each other and getting to feel, for an hour or two, anyway, a little bit less alone.

Whenever you feel lonely and desperate, as if your crisis is bigger than you are, when you're scared, when you feel as if your ordeal will overtake you, as if you're the only one in the world who's gone through anything this awful, get off your butt and get to your hearth. If you don't already have one, improvise. Go anywhere that people are gathered. Even if you don't talk to them, these strangers will bring you a blessing. Just by noticing their faces and their hands, their eyes, their weariness, their rumpled (or beautiful) clothes, their joy, the shadows of their sorrow, you will be reminded that, to one degree or another, we all feel the same things. In recognizing this connection, in experiencing it for a moment, you'll feel for a minute not quite so alone.

And if none of that does it for you, become the hearth you think you need. It has often been demonstrated — and it is in fact one of the principles of Alcoholics Anonymous — that when you give what you need, you get to keep it for yourself. Adopt a beggar, visit a hospital, become a hospice worker, record for the blind at the Braille Institute, volunteer at a nursery school, give blood. Any or all of these things can become your hearth, the place where you find communion and strength. Build a comforting hearth for others, and you, too, will feel its warmth.

Love Will Come and Find You

Remember, too, that in times of anguish and peril, there are often tiny, unexpected miracles. Ralph, for example, had been sick for more than a year. He had an esoteric brain disease that, it turned out, was a very intense allergic reaction to a food which he had been eating unawares for years. When, after his long confinement, he was finally able to leave his house, he was taken by his best friend, Sarah, to a new coffeehouse around the corner from her house. As he sat there enjoying his first cup of coffee out of captivity, a beautiful little red-haired girl moseyed up to the couch where he was sitting and started talking to him about her pink Play-Doh.

Ralph was irritated. He hadn't been out of the house for a year; he wanted to talk to Sarah, and this little girl was interrupting them. He tried to deflect her attentions, but she persisted and even boldly asked if she could sit on his lap. When she did, Ralph's heart melted. As she talked to him, asking him questions and telling him about herself, Ralph found himself quietly weeping. "It had been so long," he said to me later, "since I had paid any attention to anyone but myself, or since anyone else had paid attention to me, that it was just amazing. I had become my illness, and this beautiful little stranger welcomed me back to life."

Holy Communion

It really is too hard to go through hard times alone. At least, that's what a number of parishioners decided during a conversation after church one Sunday as they talked about their various difficult circumstances. When they heard what they were all going through, they decided to get together once a week for a common meal. The group included, among others, a therapist who'd just lost half of his clients, a small grocery store owner who was barely managing to survive after a Costco moved into town, a mother of four, a nurse who'd just left her drug-addicted husband, two young men who'd lost their part-time jobs and had to drop out of graduate school, a chemistry professor whose wife had cheated on him, and a young woman who'd been laid off from a sporting goods store because of a ski injury.

Although the meals were always simple — macaroni and cheese, chili, chicken pot pie, a salad, cheap wine, cookies for desert — the camaraderie was delicious, nourishing.

As the weeks wore on, and people's circumstances

changed, the group continued to break bread together — forming what they now call the Supper Club — in order to hold each other through the storm with their simple gift of presence. Some people's situations got better; others' got worse. One person became clinically depressed after a fruitless four-month job search, and one man even attempted suicide. Yet all the participants agree that without the support — and there isn't one of them who doesn't call it love — of one another and the group, they'd scarcely still qualify as intelligent forms of life.

Just as hard times renew our impulse to gather, nourish, and support one another, they also reach into our hearts to inspire an even greater measure of generosity. Whether your crisis finds you giving or receiving, you will find that the energy that goes along with it feels an awful lot like love.

Burning Compassion

John was incensed when he got the automated phone call telling him to vacate his house. Other people's houses might burn, the ones that were made of shingles and wood, but his house was safe. It was a big house; it had thick walls, and he "just knew" it would withstand the fire. It was only when he saw the flames licking up over the neighboring ridge that he grabbed a box of photographs and his wife's jewelry box and headed down the road.

After spending the night on an army cot in the university gym with the thirty thousand other people who were also evacuated from the fire, John realized that he wasn't so special after all. When, five days later, he returned to the bombed-out foothills and stood weeping at the ruins of his house, his "heart cracked open." He and hundreds of people around him had lost everything. He says now that he was "burned into compassion," and he suddenly realized how foolish it was to have ever imagined that he was unique or in control of anything. Everything he had had been taken away, and now he wanted to give even more. In the aftermath of the fire, he gave $100,000 to provide shelter for others who had lost their homes, and wearing shoes he was given at a downtown shelter station, he established a nonprofit organization to reforest hundreds of acres that had been decimated by the fire.

Like John, one way or another, for richer or poorer, in sickness and in health, we are gradually coming together. We don't always "learn easy." But as John teaches us, as our misery index soars, so, remarkably and beautifully, does our compassion.

Love Is All That Matters

In the end, love really is the only thing that matters. We've heard that forever, and to some degree we believe it. But do we really live it? Apart from romantic love — which, for a lot of us, consumes a great deal of our time and attention as we look everywhere for "the one" — we're not generally whiling away our afternoons just loving each other to pieces.

Why does it take a nightmare to wake us up to our need for love? Why is compassion the last thing on our agenda, after the ball game and a trip to Target, after we've answered our email and voice-mail, checked Facebook and Twitter? We have gotten so terribly far away from our gaping beautiful need for love because, somehow along the way, we have become immersed in all our distractions. Our actions often seem to indicate that we believe that things, not relationships, will nourish us; that noise, not silence, will give us peace; that electronic stimulation, not morning sunlight, will fill our souls with excitement. We have gotten so far away from the truth of our need for love that it's almost as if the cosmos itself has had to bust our chops so we would wake up and remember.

Love is relationship. It is the energy that passes between people when they are in close enough proximity — emotional, physical, spiritual — for that energy to pass between them. It is the energy, too, that passes between people and creatures, people and nature, people and the mystery. For instance, I felt that energy this morning when, pausing to meditate beside a small lake, I opened my eyes to look into the eyes of a deer who was munching the leaves from some bushes at the water's edge, and for a silent moment our spirits acknowledged each other.

Such a moment is a miracle. A miracle of love and connection and recognition. Especially in difficult times, thousands of such miracles are available, but only if we're paying attention. Longing. Hoping. Asking. Needing. Noticing. Receiving. In a sense, you could say that your crisis has been brought to you by your own need for love, and that our collective crisis has been bought to us by our collective great need for love. If this is true, and I believe it is, then if we don't respond by giving, sharing, offering, receiving, delivering, learning from, connecting through, expanding our capacity for, and showering each other with love, then this crisis shall have been in vain.

Love Is Always with You

Love is who we are. Somewhere we already know this. But the beauty of difficult times is that in them we actually get to see that love shows up in a thousand ways to hold us, that the beloved — no matter what he or she or it may look like — is always there to find us, to travel with us through our pain.

Even in the darkest hours, love will come and find you. It may not come in the way, shape, or form you imagined, but it will come to you. Like the woman standing among the stretchers on the battlefield, holding a single candle in the dark, love will surely come

and find you. Like the carpet of thin new grass spring-
ing up on the side of the fire-charred mountain, like the
raindrops of a summer thundershower sizzling on the
sidewalk after desolating months of drought, love will
come and find you.

Love is always here in our midst, and even now,
when it feels like your world is coming apart, it will
come and find you. As the mother reaches out through
the crowd for the hand of her child, love will come and
find you. As the beloved wraps his arm around his
lover's waist, as daylight wraps itself around the dark,
so love, even in these hard, dark hours, will surely
come and find you.

Love has thousands of names and millions of faces.
It will give you everything and ask for only one thing
in return — that it may come and wear your face, that
you will let it use your name.

⤝ Going Where the Love Is and You ⤞

My deep hope is that in reading about the power of
love to transform your crisis, you have been awakened
to all the startling little and immense miracles of love
that have already been brought to you in these hard
times. Here's a chance to pause for a moment and acknowledge them.

- What have been your unexpected experiences
  of love during this crisis? List them. What is

the difference they have made? For example: "Total strangers gave me their guest bedroom after our house burned down. I felt as if I'd never sleep again, and yet I felt so safe there that I know that all the other problems we have to face will be equally beautifully solved."

- What's the kind of love you still need? How would you like that to show up for you now? For example: "Physical affection and nurturing. It's been a hard haul working two jobs. I'd like to join one of those cuddle clubs, or maybe trade some of my bookkeeping for a massage."

- What is the offering of love that you would like to give? For example: "I'd like to visit soldiers in the VA hospital. I feel that they are forgotten young men and have no one to talk to about their terrible suffering."

- What, as you contemplate this offering, would be the gift that you would find yourself receiving in return? For example: "I know I would feel great gratitude. Everything I'm going through is really so basic compared to what they've been through, and what many of them will continue to struggle with for the rest of their lives."

If you want this crisis to transform you,
you will choose to

*Live in the Light
of the Spirit*

CHAPTER 10

Live in the Light of the Spirit

"On many occasions when I was dancing I have felt touched by something sacred. In those moments, I felt my spirit soar and I became one with everything that exists. I became the stars and the moon. I became the lover and the beloved. I became the victor and the vanquished...the singer and the song...the knower and the known."

—- Michael Jackson

In the remarkable works of the Dutch artist M. C. Escher, there's always a trick of artistic composition; the longer you study each work, the more surprised your eyes become. So, for example, what starts out at the top of a lithograph as clearly a bird becomes at the bottom a fish. On the surface of a single flat plane, your awareness is moved from sky to earth and then beneath the earth to the depths of the sea. Escher was fascinated with the relationships between high and low, close and near, with how our eyes behold and our consciousness perceives. Through the visual magic of his works, he invites us to notice not only that there is so much more to things than we ordinarily recognize but also that everything is beautifully and intricately related. He invites us to look at life and ourselves from an infinitely more complex and expanded view.

It's the same with what you are going through now. At the beginning, your crisis may have seemed like an unbearable tragedy, an insult from the gods, something you couldn't possibly live through. But perhaps as you have, in fact, found yourself moving through it a single day, a single breath at a time, you've started to get a sense of its deeper meaning. That's because one of the gifts of crisis is that it always holds the seeds of seeing life and ourselves in a new and larger frame.

The most profound gift of any crisis — its backbone, heart, and brain — is that it calls us to restructure ourselves along spiritual lines. But just as we don't always operate from love in comfortable times, we don't always live from an awareness of our spirits either.

Our spirits are that which is eternal in us, that which abides beyond life. Your spirit is energy itself, the energy that causes us to be here; it is you, and it is what shall remain of you when your days in the shadow-dance of life are over. It's easy to become disengaged with our spirits because life is compelling and the material universe endlessly enchanting and demanding. We can literally spend all our time engaged with our stuff, our dreams, our Life Themes, and our current taxing stories without ever stumbling into the realm of spirit.

One of the functions of crisis is to take us exactly there, to that greater awareness. It joggles us into knowing that we are more than people living so-called human lives. Difficulties get us to experience, rather than just mouth, the truth — that we are spiritual beings who are having this experience. A spiritual life is that place in our consciousness where we acknowledge the mystery, holiness, oneness, and union-through-spirit of us all.

A Spiritual Wake-Up Call

"A spiritual wake-up call." That's what Lauren said after her shocking and sudden divorce. Her husband told her one day, served her with papers the next, and was gone on the third. Three weeks later, he was arrested in another state for thirteen felonies and discovered to have a police record a mile long. In the space of one month, not only was Lauren faced with the loss of her husband, but she was also stripped of any sense whatsoever that she had ever really known him. Worse yet, she was left with the feeling that she

had never known or correctly judged anyone or anything.

At first she felt totally crazed, but as she lived moment by moment, day by day, through this near-
insanity-making crisis — weeping, moving out of the
house, finding a job, meditating, praying — she gradually began to see it in a larger framework. She saw
that her marriage, her husband, her perceptions, and
even her life itself were not all there is. She realized
that through this crisis, she was being asked to surrender to the soul-wide truth that this life is simply one
expression of something much larger. Step by step
through her anguishing journey she saw that in spite of
the gigantic sweep of her losses, there was something
unchangeable and untouched in her that remained.

As she inhabited this new sense of herself, feeling
disoriented at times, feeling life to be almost bizarre
and irrelevant, she gradually began to connect to every
person whose path she crossed, as if, somehow, mys-
teriously she partook of everything that they had ever
gone through. "I don't really know how to express it,"
she said, "except to say that I felt a part of everything
and everyone. It was as if my personality receded and
then was practically erased. Nothing seemed to matter in the way it had before, and yet it all seemed infinitely precious. It was almost as if I was hardly in this
reality, although I was functioning perfectly. I felt as if
I was inside life and beyond it, both at once." She said,

too, that when this feeling of simultaneous presence and transcendence finally subsided, she felt a deep sense of peace, and that despite the ordinary tasks and stresses of life, this peace has remained.

The same enlightening awareness is available to you. Along with feeling simple gratitude for the fact that you've managed to survive your particular ordeal, you may notice that your consciousness is expanding. Instead of being stranded at the level of fretting about all the things you can no longer afford, you may find yourself in awe of the single blade of grass that has insisted itself through a crack in the sidewalk. Instead of focusing on what you've lost — the relationship, the car, the lifestyle, plans for the future suddenly smashed to bits — maybe you're strangely, miraculously at peace. You find yourself gratefully residing in a single unrepeatable moment in which your breath, in its unutterable simplicity and constancy, trumpets the astonishing fact that you are alive, that without intending it or knowing exactly how, your soul, in some infinite eternal lottery, was the winner of the jackpot of one human life.

Crisis is the crucible of expanded awareness because it gets us to respond to life in ways that are not patterned or familiar. It changes our energy, pushes our emotions around, taxes our bodies, gives us sleepless nights and heartache, so that our very physical structures and our psyches are vulnerable to information and perceptions that ordinarily elude us. When we are taken apart at the seams, we are vulnerable and permeable; our structures are out of sync enough, revised enough, flimsy enough to entertain some new information. We are open. We can be changed. And we do change.

The Car Years

Mindy is now a very successful woman with her own internet consulting business. But not long ago through a complex set of circumstances — which included the death of her parents, a life-threatening illness, and gigantic financial reversals — she ended up living in her car for two years. When she talks about "the car years," as she calls them, it's without shame or regret; in fact, there's almost longing in her voice.

She told me that she had never felt so whole, that every day was a day of grace, that when the sun "roared in" through her car windows each morning, she felt a wild exuberance simply about still being alive. The kindness of the people she met at the thrift store where she bought (and often had to sell back) her clothes was amazing, and the generosity of strangers who gave her food, let her come to their houses so she could shower, and utilized her talents in their businesses until she could get on her feet was "breathtaking." She says she was "so close to the edge" that at times she almost could see "the entire structure of the universe"; though it had been invisible to her before, she could now see that everything was related to everything else. Day by day everything she asked for was granted, each of her needs fulfilled.

There were times, too, during these two years, when she would go out in the world and the world itself would seem to be bathed in white light, would seem to be real and unreal, both at once. The first few times this happened she wondered if she were nuts, crazed from not having had enough to eat, but she began to see this as a gift, a privileged view of the veils between existence.

Mindy is grateful now for her house, her car, and a successful career, but she says that her years in the car were the most blessed days of her life. As a consequence of what she "learned in the car," she has made a lifelong commitment to dedicate half of her earnings to at-risk youth. She knows from the inside that without help many of them will never get beyond the kind of poverty that takes young lives apart.

Crisis and the Sacred: A Spiritual Opportunity

The relationship between the human creature and eternity has always been known by those great souls whose natural province is the connection between this life and all of consciousness. Shamans, medicine men, aborigines, saints, mystics, artists, and enlightened beings of all times have always seen the relationship between timelessness and the measured increments of time created by the human mind.

In one way or another, they have all been telling us that there is more. There is more to you than what you ordinarily think of as yourself, more to existence than what you ordinarily think of as your life. These spiritually accomplished people did not receive this advanced awareness by driving BMWs or eating at McDonald's. They came to it through various forms, all of them involving a divine tapping on the shoulder — after years of sitting in meditation, through a near-death experience or the loss of everything and everyone dear to them, through grueling physical disciplines or sometimes being quite literally struck by lightning.

In a similar — though, I hope, slightly less dramatic — way, the crisis you are going through is your personal invitation to come to an awareness of what these sages have always known. It is your chance to become acquainted with that which is larger than life, that which is eternal in you. Often that change comes in the form of a breakthrough perception, when you stumble for no reason — but, of course, for every divine and eternal reason — into an instant of breathtaking joy so extraordinary and stunning that suddenly you know that you yourself and even life itself are not all there is.

Sometimes, of course, this happens when everything is going well in life. Some people experience it dancing or sky diving, others through the ongoing disciplined practice of meditation, still others in moments of sexual ecstasy, intervals of such precious seamless connection that the distance between self and other is erased and there is a feeling of melting, of having dissolved. Far more often it comes as a fruit of anguish, great grief, huge loss, physical suffering so exquisite that it bounces you out of your body for a moment and you realize, clearly and forever, that you are not your body but something beyond a physical self.

In such moments, our perception of everything we have run after and struggled for is suddenly reorganized. It's not that the things of this world no longer matter. You're still here on earth. Tomorrow, again, you'll need gas for the car, cream for your coffee, money to pay the electric bill. But for just a moment, instead of being consumed by life's details, you can see them as the elaborate and amusing movements of a chess game, which is played on a table in a huge living room with a vaulted ceiling so high that you can scarcely see it. Life is that chessboard, our human experience the movement of the pieces, and the living room the eternal context in which our lives occur.

These gifts of transcendent awareness — of heaven on earth — are not likely to arrive when you're shopping at Macy's — unless perhaps you have a heart attack at the cosmetics counter and find yourself keeling over and into the realm of white light. They are far more likely to occur when you can no longer take refuge in the familiar structures or mechanisms of everyday life, when you are, in effect, railroaded by crisis itself to get off the chessboard and fly to the limits of the vaulted ceiling. In such moments, just as we are caught off guard by the eye-catching transformations in an Escher lithograph, we are likely to find that the ribs of the vaulted ceiling are an optical illusion, that there is actually only endless space at the top of the room, and that, in fact, the room never had any walls.

Signs of a Sea Change

What is especially beautiful about the crisis you're in is that it's not just happening to you. It's also happening to my friend who visited from Europe, to the people standing next to you in the grocery store or pumping gas at the island next to you. It's happening to the thousands of people who have lost their jobs, to the people who lost their money to Madoff, to those who lost their houses to fires and floods and tornadoes. It's happening to the owners of failed businesses and bankrupt restaurant chains, to world economies teetering on the brink of collapse. It's happening to rich and poor alike in countries all over the globe.

Hardly anybody alive can keep from noticing that big change is in the air. We can smell it, feel it, taste it. Entire ways of being are ending. Like a Labrador retriever, sauntering out of the water after a long, strong swim, we are shaking off the water of the old. Shimmering drops of the way things used to be are scattering like thousands of diamonds around us. Your difficult time and mine and all of ours is happening because it must, because the old has to end for the new to begin.

Of course, we are scared, even terrified, as we watch the old ways disappear. But just as the vast black void of the universe is endlessly spawning new stars, which in turn explode into supernovas, rebirth is happening everywhere around us, and what you can only call a new consciousness, a new way of being, is slowly rising in our midst.

Hundreds of artifacts of modern civilization — television sets with rabbit ears, telephones with dials, vinyl records, disc jockeys, Woolworth's, mom-and-pop corner grocery stores, even Dodger stadium — have disappeared or transformed while we were scarcely paying attention. The world is changing. Old things are falling away. New things have already taken root in our midst. The internet, an amazing new organism of consciousness, is bringing us ever more deeply together. Vast tendrils of connection are being delivered through the ubiquity of the cell phone. Through the pulsating connectivity of the web, we can read the wisdom of the ages, diagnose our own health problems, connect with people we haven't spoken to for decades, find new friends among strangers, and meet the husbands and wives of our dreams. Like the new nervous system of humanity, it is connecting us to the distant limbs of the collective organism that we are, and this profound opportunity for connection is practically a spiritual imperative.

The internet isn't just a way to while away our afternoons and evenings with more entertainment, nor is it simply the key to a paperless world; it is the electric pulsating presence of our connectedness. It is a request from the universe that we expand the reach of our love, the recognition of our oneness.

A woman named Kelly found her husband-to-be, a man with the same first and last names as hers, by fiddling around with Google one night. My friend Mary was suddenly overtaken by the impulse to look up an old friend; after spending hours on the internet, she located him in a city a hundred miles away and was able to be with him the final weeks before he died. Another friend established a website where thousands of schoolchildren from around the world, many living in such remote places they scarcely have a concept of the world, can now communicate with one another. America's first African American president got elected in part because of his internet savvy. Within a week six million people had heard the astonishing voice of a shy Scottish woman, Susan Boyle, who for years had lived alone with her cat, Pebbles, and hundreds of millions of people were moved, even after his death, by the mesmerizing dance steps of Michael Jackson.

We are increasingly seeing, feeling, and experiencing how unavoidably connected we all are. And we're not just connected in the present. We can also be carried backward in time, to the music of the sixties, the sonnets of Shakespeare, the Anglo-Saxon epic poem *Beowulf* — all of which we can see and read and hear online. In the past in order to see such things, you would have to actually go to the British Museum or the pyramids. But now, with the flick of a finger, you can partake of them in cyberspace. Boundaries are melting. Time is drooping over our chairs like Dalí watches. We are leaning in, feeling, finding each other.

We don't have a choice about all this interconnectedness. We can't go back to the way things were. Our task now is simply to respond, to awaken to the experience of communion that is making its way to us, through us.

On a practical level, as we have already seen, this new experience is one of collaboration — we find ourselves helping each other. On the level of consciousness it is one of an expanded awareness of union, of the truth that we are all inextricably and utterly connected, that, indeed, through the mystery of spirit, we are one. The mechanics of this new awareness are also different; we live differently as we embody the awareness of union, the realization that we are all part of one another.

Intuition, forgiveness, presence — these are the hallmarks of this new consciousness in our midst. Instead of selfishness, narcissism, and greed, we are in the mood for sharing. Instead of analyzing, thinking, figuring things out, we are operating from intuition. Instead of conflict and domination, we are seeking an experience of presence. And instead of being motivated by judgment, grudges, and revenge, we are looking for the doorway to forgiveness.

More Than Forty Years in the Wilderness

Half a century ago, Elwin Wilson, who kept a black doll hanging from a noose outside his home, was one of a gang of white men who attacked black Freedom Riders and left one of them, John Lewis, who is today a US congressman, beaten and bloodied on the ground outside a South Carolina bus station.

For years, Wilson said, he had tried to block the incident out of his mind. Then, one day a year ago he was asked casually by a friend where he thought he would go after he died. When he heard himself say "probably to hell," this dyed-in-the-wool racist decided it was time to apologize. He sought out the man he had bloodied and assaulted, and, words breaking through tears, asked for forgiveness with a simple, "I'm sorry." Lewis graciously accepted Wilson's apology, and Wilson says he is now at peace and that he hopes his own quest for redemption will inspire others to step forward and heal the wounds they have created. "If just one person comes forward and gets the hate out of their heart, it's all worth it," he said.

Forgiveness isn't tangible. It doesn't change anything, except on a spiritual level. Like the change in Wilson's heart, and the bond of peace that now exists between him and the man he once bloodied on the sidewalk, transactions in the life of the spirit — forgiveness, presence, intuition — are nothing you can grab hold of. They are mysterious, sacred, invisible. But in our hearts and souls we know, beyond a shadow of a doubt, when we have been transformed by them.

The Path to Peace

The journey of spirit is always a deep one, and it may not be apparent to others, but only to one's inner eye. So it was for Mark, who came home one night from a business trip to find that his wife of fourteen years had moved out, lock, stock, and barrel, leaving not a trace of her presence. Mark fell apart for three days, then recognized that this was an invitation to develop his spiritual life. Two days later, in the airport on yet another business trip, he passed dozens of Tibetan monks wearing red robes. He took this as a sign that he needed to move in the direction of spiritual practice and contemplation.

Returning home, Mark trained in meditation, and he has continued his practice for the past seven years.

He says that through this process, everything has changed. He hasn't found a new wife, and he recently lost his job. But through his meditation practice he is able to arrive at a place of "the deepest tranquility imaginable," one in which the usual concerns of his life seem almost like amusements, images that pass across a movie screen.

Our crises invite us to develop a spiritual practice, not just as a momentary diversion, but as a way of living. Disruption suggests that we incorporate a practice of silence, of presence, of gratitude that will allow us to see in every moment, not just when our worlds are falling apart, that there is so much more to life and to ourselves than we ordinarily imagine. We need a spiritual practice not because times are hard but because life is hard. The whole point of the journey of our lives is to get us, one way or another, in touch with this greater dimension.

That is the call.

You can do this, as Mark did, through the practice of meditation; as Michael Jackson did, through dancing; or as Edmund Hillary and Tenzing Norgay did, by climbing Mount Everest. You can do it through the practice of yoga, through lovingkindness meditation, through surfing or walking on the beach. However you do it, the outcome will always be to take you beyond what is present and of this world and into a sense that you and life are much larger than you ever imagined.

The fruit of a spiritual life is always tranquility. Your crisis is inviting you to find that peace.

The Truth of Who We Are

Spiritual life gives us a shimmering new awareness that this life is not the whole of things. As we move through the paces of our spiritual practice, we begin to hear the whispers deep inside us. Gradually we come to know, to remember, that there is something deeper and more ancient in us, something forever-ish at our core, something that was and will always be, something whose scope is vast and whose breath is eternal, something that we call god or spirit or soul.

In moments of crisis, especially, we see this. The veil opens and finally we can hear the song that has been traveling thousands of years through the darkness to find us. Suddenly, we can feel our souls, and we know we can trust this deepest part of ourselves. The eternal silence, the infinite light, embraces us, and we know that we are not just people stranded on earth with our heartaches. Each one of us is a fragment of the divine eternal awareness that is consciousness itself. For a moment we remember that we are eternal, all-capable, all-encompassing. The energy that we are is vast — bodiless light, and Love itself — and it will go on forever. Like the birds at the top of an Escher lithograph that become fish at the bottom, this crisis and even you yourself will be transformed, and only the love that you are will remain.

In the face of all that, doesn't whatever you're going through seem a little bit easier? Think of it as a temporary setback. Someday it will be over, but you, your essence, your spirit, your love, will go on. *We* go on. The love that we are goes on.

Don't ask me how I know that.

I just do.

❧ Living in the Light of the Spirit and You ❧

In ways you may not be aware of, your spiritual life is already alive inside you. Taking note of it, nurturing it, bringing it just a little bit more to the forefront of your consciousness will bring you the peace your crisis is asking you to find.

- What experience or experiences have you had that connected you to your own transcendent and eternal nature? Do you think of these experiences as weird and not to be taken seriously, or do you allow them to encourage and comfort you? How have these experiences changed your view of life?

- Think about your current crisis for a moment and ask yourself the following question: A hundred years from now, what difference will this make?

- Do you have a daily spiritual practice, and what is it? If not, when do you engage the life of the spirit? Walking by the ocean or watching the sunset? Running? Doing Yoga? Listening to music or dancing? Meditating? Having precious exchanges with your children? Would you be willing to make any of these a daily practice? Can you feel the spiritual strength this might give you? When would you like to begin?

PEACE BE WITH YOU

～

May the depth of your crisis remind you of who you really are. May your pain bring you into the light of awareness. May your journey through it give you hope. And when you have made it through the storm, may you feel great peace and joy.

ACKNOWLEDGMENTS

Without the loving presence and help of my fellow travelers, this book would have remained only an idea.

Thanks to all the people at New World Library — especially the company's visionary publisher, Marc Allen — for recognizing that now is the time for this message. My deep thanks to Georgia Hughes, my editor, for vision and great steadiness of heart and mind as the journey of this book unfolded. Also, and very especially, great and loving thanks to Mary Jane Ryan, who yet again, with patience, gratitude, and generosity, accompanied me on the journey. You are a treasure in my life. I was blessed by the hospitality of John McCauley and Suntah Oannes in Maui during the early stages of the writing; by the folks at Zaca Lake, and that one beautiful deer, as I completed the manuscript. Love and thanks to Carol Lingham and Eric Lassen for their everyday lovingkindness as I labored, fretted, and prevailed. And much happy love to Molly, who always keeps me real and true.

I acknowledge you too — out there, whoever you are — because surely, more than ever before, we know that we're all in this together; and I have heard your cry. I would not have written this book, and you would not be reading it, had we not come to some deep new challenges and the opportunity to rise through them with our hearts and souls intact. Bless each one of you.

Finally, I acknowledge that although I am the one who sits at the computer and taps at the little black keys, I am really only the secretary for that which speaks through me. I bow in gratitude for having been chosen to write these words.

ABOUT THE AUTHOR

An inspirational author, relationship coach, and spiritual guide, Daphne Rose Kingma is the author of eleven books on love and relationships, including the bestsellers *Coming Apart*, *The Men We Never Knew*, *True Love*, *The Future of Love*, and *Loving Yourself*. Her books have sold more than one million copies and been translated into fifteen languages.

For more than two decades Daphne has worked with individuals and couples to enhance the quality of their relationships and bring more love into their lives. Dubbed the "Love Doctor" by the *San Francisco Chronicle*, she created the Relationship Intensive, a highly personalized workshop tailored to meet the needs of individual couples.

Since 2008 she has applied the principles covered in this book in working with people in various kinds of life crises. Based on this work, she created Making It Through, a workshop that offers people a process for not only living through but being transformed by the crises they are in.

Daphne has been a frequent guest on *Oprah*. She has also appeared on numerous other television shows and networks, including *Charlie Rose* and CNN, as well as hundreds of radio programs. Her work has appeared in a host of newspapers and magazines, including the *Los Angeles Times*, *Mademoiselle*, *Self*, the *St. Louis Post-Dispatch*, and the *Dallas Morning News*. A highly sought-after speaker, she presents keynotes to audiences throughout the United States and in Europe and regularly conducts workshops for the Esalen Institute in Big Sur, California, and the Recreer Foundation in Paris, France. She lives in Santa Barbara, California.

To learn more or to inquire about keynotes, personal consultation, the Relationship Intensive, or Making It Through, visit

www.daphnekingma.com.

NEW WORLD LIBRARY is dedicated to publishing books and other media that inspire and challenge us to improve the quality of our lives and the world.

We are a socially and environmentally aware company, and we strive to embody the ideals presented in our publications. We recognize that we have an ethical responsibility to our customers, our staff members, and our planet.

We serve our customers by creating the finest publications possible on personal growth, creativity, spirituality, wellness, and other areas of emerging importance. We serve New World Library employees with generous benefits, significant profit sharing, and constant encouragement to pursue their most expansive dreams.

As a member of the Green Press Initiative, we print an increasing number of books with soy-based ink on 100 percent postconsumer-waste recycled paper. Also, we power our offices with solar energy and contribute to nonprofit organizations working to make the world a better place for us all.

Our products are available
in bookstores everywhere.
For our catalog, please contact:

New World Library
14 Pamaron Way
Novato, California 94949

Phone: 415-884-2100 or 800-972-6657
Catalog requests: Ext. 50
Orders: Ext. 52
Fax: 415-884-2199
Email: escort@newworldlibrary.com
To subscribe to our electronic newsletter, visit
www.newworldlibrary.com